The Ku Klux Klan
In American Politics

The Ku Klux Klan
In American Politics

By ARNOLD S. RICE

INTRODUCTION BY HARRY GOLDEN

HASKELL HOUSE PUBLISHERS Ltd.
Publishers of Scarce Scholarly Books
NEW YORK, N. Y. 10012
1972

Library of Congress Cataloging in Publication Data

Rice, Arnold S
    The Ku Klux Klan in American politics.

    Bibliography: p.
    1. Ku-Klux Klan (1915-   ) 2. U. S.--
Politics and government--20th century. I. Title.
[HS2330.K63R5 1972]   322.4'3   72-1152
ISBN 0-8383-1427-9

Printed in the United States of America

INTRODUCTION

There is something quite frightening about this book. It is not so much that Dr. Rice recounts some of the brutalities and excesses of the Ku Klux Klan or even that he measures the intelligence of those who led the cross-burners as wanting; indeed, those of us who lived through the "kleagling" of the 1920's remember that the Klansmen, while not men, weren't boys either. What is frightening is the amount of practical action the successors to the Klan have learned from it. They have learned not only from the Klan's mistakes but from the Klan's successes.

Fortunately, neither the John Birch Society nor the White Citizens Councils nor the revivified Klan nor the McCarthyites have learned well enough to grasp ultimate power. All of them, however, have learned enough so that they are more than an annoyance to the democratic process.

Just how successful was the Klan? It never played a crucial role in a national election. The presence of Klansmen on the floor of a national political convention often succeeded in watering down the anti-Klan plank but national candidates, if they chose, could castigate the Klan at will. In the presidential campaign of 1928 between Alfred E. Smith and Herbert Hoover, the Klan helped bring the virulency of anti-Catholicism to a fever point, but that virulency was always there and it was not strictly that virulency which lost Al Smith the White House. True, Klan propaganda may have helped Smith lose the electoral votes of five traditionally Democratic Southern states but Republicans and prosperity really dealt him the loss. If Daniel Boone had been running on the Democratic ticket in 1928 he would have been swamped, too.

Nor was the Klan ever notably successful in state politics. Their politicking rarely won consistent effects and often resulted in abject failure: vide Dr. Rice's summary of the election of "Ma" Ferguson in Texas in the mid 1920's. The Klan dissipated, says Dr. Rice. There were too many politicians among them and of those politicians too many were simply stupid. But where the Klan was successful was in local politics. In many Southern States, in Indiana, Ohio, and New Jersey, at the precinct level the Klan was not only a potent political force, it was the electorate. Whole police departments were composed of Klansmen and the municipal committees were composed of Klansmen and the mayor and the dog catcher, if not Klansmen too, were dependent upon Klansmen's favor.

The Klan was most successful when it espoused Americanism rather than specific candidates at the state and national level. The John Birch Society which inundates its secret cells with a continuous flow of reading material learned this from the Klan; and the White Citizens Councils, whom Hodding Carter calls the "uptown Klan", imitate the Klan when they solicit doctors and other professional men before starting their larger recruiting drive for members.

Why then do they never succeed to ultimate power?

They fail really because they themselves become a national issue before they can create a national issue to their liking. The Klansmen loved tar and feathering, floggings, kidnappings and night riding expeditions. Thus, they made violence a national issue. The White Citizens Councils did not move to disperse the mobs which congregated around the public schools when the lone Negro child walked into it and they too made mob action not only a national but an international issue. Because they are a secret society the John Birch Society has made the mistake no public society would ever have committed: Robert Welch, their leader, called Dwight D. Eisenhower and John Foster Dulles Communists (to my mind Mr. Welch is a lot like the old-fashioned hoopskirt in that he covers everything but touches nothing). And the late Senator Joe McCarthy became a national issue because he was a Republican in a Republican Administration and while I am aware that the decency and honesty of the politicians received the bravos for discrediting him, I believe the instinct for self-preservation, which runs high in all politicians, should get some share of this glory, too.

Dr. Rice, whose book is economical yet inclusive, offers up several reasons why men did don silly robes and masks and burn crosses on the hillside. They are all cogent and I do not wish to anticipate his way of telling his story, but, in conclusion, I would like to touch on one reason he does not mention.

America was the first moral idea among nations and being an American is a heady moral experience. It is so heady an experience that literally it drives some people insane. The experience is too much for them and they don foolish costumes and invent an equally foolish nomenclature and yet, possibly because their wellsprings are American, they manage for a short while, to terrorize the rest of us. We had best understand them.

HARRY GOLDEN

Charlotte, North Carolina

PREFACE

The Ku Klux Klan of the twentieth century has been a many-sided organization. Comprising its creed have been a half dozen or so tenets. To carry out its program based upon these articles of faith, the secret order has used a variety of political methods. Unfortunately, the Klan has left the scantiest amount of documentary evidence concerning its activities. For this reason no work on the Klan—including this one—can pretend to be truly comprehensive.

Contrary to general belief, Klanism has been nationwide. In practically every state of the union there have existed local chapters. Indeed, on the Pacific coast and in the Middle West in the 1920's the secret order achieved tremendous power and success. Nevertheless, it is a matter of historical record that the Klan has been predominantly a southern phenomenon. The brain of the Klan, the heart of the Klan are stamped "Dixie." Therefore, this work necessarily lays stress on Klanism in the South.

As used herein the term "the South" refers to thirteen states—the eleven states that comprised the Confederacy plus two of the border slave states which held for the Union during the Civil War, Maryland and Kentucky. While the other border slave states of 1861-1865, Delaware and Missouri, and the post-bellum state Oklahoma are sometimes considered with West Virginia to be a part of the twentieth century South, Klan influence in those states has not been strong enough to warrant detailed treatment.

The period from 1915 to the present is covered herein. Both ceremonially and legally, 1915 marks the beginning of the secret order patterned after the Ku Klux Klan of Reconstruction days. In a sense 1960 is of terminal significance since a Catholic was chosen President of the United States despite all the efforts of the Klan to prevent his election.

The progress of the author's research was greatly hampered by the Klan's secrecy. Moreover, because the organization has been discredited, former Klansmen have been unwilling to discuss with outsiders their recollections of the inner workings of the order. In addition, the personal papers of ex-Klansmen relating to their activities in the fraternity have either been destroyed or kept hidden. Thus writing this book has been far from easy.

Happily, many individuals have given me generous assistance—journalists and historians, librarians who made every effort to satisfy my requests for source materials, fellow teachers who read individual chapters and commented thereon, relatives and friends who gave me lodging while I was away from home doing research. But there are two people to whom I owe especial thanks for the completion of this book. One is Dr. Chase C. Mooney, Associate Professor of History at Indiana University. A critic extraordinary, he always counselled, never prescribed. The other is Marcia Griff Rice, my wife. As research assistant, grammarian, and literary stylist, she contributed vastly more than a husband had the right to expect.

ARNOLD S. RICE

Colonia, New Jersey

CONTENTS

Chapter I

HISTORICAL BACKGROUND

On Thanksgiving night, 1915, sixteen men motored from Atlanta, Georgia, to nearby Stone Mountain, a six hundred and fifty foot dome-shaped rising of solid gray granite. Stumbling in the dark on the steep, smooth stone trail, the men worked their way slowly to the broad top of the mountain. There, braving the "surging blasts of wild wintry mountain winds and . . . a temperature far below freezing,"[1] they quickly and quietly carried out their appointed tasks. Soon the small group found itself gathered under a burning wooden cross and before a hastily constructed rock altar upon which lay an American flag, an opened Bible, an unsheathed sword, and a canteen of water. A sacred oath of allegiance was taken to the Invisible Empire, Knights of the Ku Klux Klan.

William Joseph Simmons of Atlanta was the leader that night. A month before, on October 16, 1915, after hearing him outline his plans for a fraternity patterned after the Ku Klux Klan of Reconstruction days, thirty-four Georgians had put their signatures to an application to the authorities of their state for a charter. On December 4, 1915, a week after that night on top of Stone Mountain, the charter was granted. Professedly an eleemosynary organization, it was formally defined as a "patriotic, secret, social, benevolent order under the name and style of 'Knights of the Ku Klux Klan.'" On July 1, 1916, on petition of Simmons and eleven others, the order was duly incorporated by the Superior Court of Fulton County, Georgia.

What of Simmons' past? Rather little of his life before 1915 is definitely known. He was born, it appears, in 1880, on a farm near Harpersville, Alabama, where he spent his childhood. After serving in the Spanish-American War as a private in an Alabama regiment, he became a circuit rider of the Methodist Episcopal Church. After a decade or so of ministerial work, he turned to selling, drifting from one job to another.[2] In or about 1912 he accepted a post as instructor in Southern history at Lanier University in Atlanta.

An important aspect of Simmons' career throughout his early adult years was his not too successful recruiting or "boosting" for various fraternal orders. Fraternalism was something quite dear to him. With a measure of pride, he once declared:

"I am a member of a number of fraternal orders — the Masons, Royal Arch Masons, the Great Order of Knight Templars, and . . . [other] affiliations that I have gone into, about twelve or fifteen in number, in my lifetime. . . . In fact, I have been a fraternalist ever since I was in the academy school way back yonder and I believe in fraternal orders and fraternal relationships among men, in a fraternity of nations, so that all people might know something of the great doctrine of the fatherhood of God and the brotherhood of man."[3]

What of Simmons' personal characteristics? Tall and lanky, he was auburn-haired, smooth-shaven, clear-eyed behind the pince-nez perched upon a prominent nose, thin-lipped, and deep-voiced. Possessed of a spellbinding rhetoric, he talked like the old-time revivalist preacher he resembled. His pleasures, however, were anything but clerical — horse races, boxing matches, "social" drinking.

"Colonel" Simmons — he gloried in this title[4] — was a person of deep emotions. Whenever he read or heard tales of the Ku Klux Klan he seems to have been in a true state of pleasure. "From a child in dresses," he once related, "I can remember how old Aunt Viney, my black mammy, used to pacify us children late in the evening by telling us about the Kuklux." With wide eyes and open mouth he listened to others (among whom was his father, a bona fide member of the first Klan) tell stories about the Reconstruction organization. Late one night, in his twentieth year, while he was perusing a newly found book about the Klan, a vision suddenly appeared to him: "On horseback in their white robes they [the Klansmen of old] rode across the wall in front of me, and as the picture faded out I got down on my knees and swore that I would found a fraternal organization which would be a memorial to the Ku Klux Klan." For fifteen years Simmons never forgot his great vow. On Thanksgiving night, 1915, on top of Stone Mountain the moment arrived. He could then well say: " . . . the Invisible Empire was called from its slumber of half a century to take up a new task."

Although "Colonel" Simmons' Klan was to be a memorial to the original organization, it came to possess a wider program than its precursor. To the Reconstruction order's anti-Negroism, the twentieth century Klan soon added anti-Catholicism, anti-Semitism, and anti-foreign-bornism. But if the new Klan was more than the old in program, it copied its forerunner in structure. The revived Invisible Empire, coextensive with the United States, was divided into eight

"Domains," each comprised of anywhere from a single thickly populated state (such as the "Domain of the East" which contained only
New York) to a half dozen or so sparsely populated neighboring states
(such as the "Domain of the Mississippi Valley" which included seven
states). Each one of the forty-eight states, known as a "Realm," was
further broken down into "Provinces," most of which held a score or
so of counties. Within each Province lay the smallest units in the
Invisible Empire, the individual "Klans" or local chapters.[5]

The Invisible Empire was under the rule of the "Imperial Wizard,"
the Domain under the command of the "Grand Goblin," the Realm
under the jurisdiction of the "Grand Dragon," the Province under the
control of the "Great Titan," and the local Klan under the leadership
of the "Exalted Cyclops."

"Colonel" Simmons was the first Imperial Wizard of the Ku Klux
Klan. As such, his edicts were to be respected throughout each and
every division of the Invisible Empire. He had the sole power of
appointment to, and removal from, his cabinet of twelve Imperial officers, who were known collectively as the "Genii." No charter could
be granted to a local Klan without his consent, and any charter could
be revoked upon his request. Moreover, he was the sole formulator
of all ritual and the sole arbiter of all dogma of the Knights of the Ku
Klux Klan. Coadjutor to the Imperial Wizard was the "Emperor."
His job was largely one of expediting all transactions coming from the
"Imperial Aulic," or sanctum, of the Imperial Wizard. The office of
Emperor was set up in 1922 to satisfy the "Colonel's" desire for an
administrative assistant.

The Imperial legislature of the Ku Klux Klan was called the "Klonvokation." Meeting biennially or at the request of the Imperial Wizard,
this body was composed of the Imperial Wizard, the Emperor, the
Genii, and the presiding officer of each subdivision of the Invisible
Empire. Advising the Imperial Wizard and the Klonvokation was
the "Kloncilium." Assembling annually or during an emergency in
a special session called by the Imperial Wizard, the Kloncilium con-
sisted of the Genii and any other Klansmen asked to serve. Primarily
a judicial body, the Kloncilium could also act legislatively whenever
the Klonvokation was not in session.

Because the constitution of the Klan provided no clear definition
of the particular duties and prerogatives of the three organs of the
Imperial division — the Imperial Wizard and his Genii, the Klonvokation, and the Kloncilium — confusion and conflict existed during the
reign of Imperial Wizard Simmons. As the reign of Simmons' suc-

cessor wore on, both the Klonvokation and Kloncilium became merely the extended arm of the Imperial Wizard.

With each Domain doing little besides existing on paper, and with its Grand Goblin being little more than a sinecurist, the first important subdivision below the Imperial sphere was the Realm with its Grand Dragon. Each Grand Dragon was the Imperial Wizard's personal representative in the Realm, appointed by him and removed at his will. Assisting each Grand Dragon in carrying out unhesitatingly the commands of the Imperial Wizard was a council of nine, known collectively as the "Hydras."

One of the Grand Dragon's powers was to subdivide his Realm into Provinces and to appoint, without confirmation from his superiors, a Great Titan to each. Attached to the presiding officer of each Province was a group of seven advisors, the "Furies." Set up for recruitment purposes, the Province was permitted to exist long after it had fulfilled its original function. Occupying the layer it did in the strata of authority within the Invisible Empire, the vestigial Province prevented direct contact between the Realm officers and the local Klans, a situation quite detrimental to the efficient execution of Imperial decrees in the farthest reaches of the Invisible Empire.

Members of the local Klan, with the consent of both the Great Titan and the Grand Dragon of the Province and the Realm directly concerned, elected their own officers. They were, in addition to the Exalted Cyclops, eleven "Terrors," the "Klaliff" (Vice-President), the "Klokard" (Lecturer), the "Kludd" (Chaplain), the "Kligrapp" (Secretary), the "Klabee" (Treasurer), the "Kladd" (Conductor of members into the meeting), the "Klarogo" (Inner Guard of the meeting), the "Klexter" (Outer Guard of the meeting), and the three "Klokann" (a Board of Investigators, Auditors, and Advisors, each member of which bore the title "Klokan").

The meeting place of a local Klan was called the "Klavern." Any room could serve as such if it were properly decked out with an altar upon which lay an American flag (to show the patriotism of those present), a Bible open at Romans XII (as a guide to the Christian life), an unsheathed sword (representing the determination to overcome the obstacles to Christian living), and a container of water (the contents of which were sprinkled upon initiates to rid them of "alien" defilement), and if it were illuminated by a "fiery cross" (best known symbol of the organization, made usually of wood and electric light bulbs, which was said to have been inspired by the burning crosses that rallied the Scottish clans). The Klan was required to hold a meeting, called a "Klonklave," at least once a month, with six "Knights" (members of the order) constituting a quorum. Each meeting was conducted according to the order set forth in the "Kloran," the official manual on Klonklave procedure. To outsiders the rubric of the Klonklave would certainly have appeared tiresomely long; the opening ceremony, for example, filled eight closely printed pages of the Kloran, while the closing ceremony filled five.[6]

Four years before that Thanksgiving night on top of Stone Mountain, "Colonel" Simmons, confined to his bed following an automobile accident, had ample time to ruminate about other aspects of his dream organization besides its native-born, white, Protestant philosophy and subdivisional structure. Indeed, while he lay bedridden for three months he was able to work out most of the details for the costume consisting of the peaked hood and robe, the various emblems and tokens,[7] the placing of the letters "Kl" in front of every title, the ritual of the local Klan meeting, and the motto, "Non Silba Sed Anthar."[8]

For the first few years after receiving its charter, the Klan had an uneventful, if not precarious, existence. Dogged by a lack of financial backing and only half-hearted co-operation from his fellow Knights, Imperial Wizard Simmons carried on almost single-handed. It was he who did the recruiting, saw to the advertising, arranged for the production of regalia, and drafted the constitution.[9] Of those early years of adversity, the "Colonel" was wont to reminisce aloud—and none too modestly — of his perseverance:

". . . the work was a tremendous struggle, made more arduous by a traitor in our ranks who held under me a position of trust, who embezzled all of our accumulated funds in the summer of 1916 . . . The treacherous conduct of this man left me penniless, with a large accumulation of debts against the order. I was advised to give it up by many, but I felt and knew that my honor was at stake. . . . I was forced to mortgage my home in order to get money with which to carry on . . . the work we had to do.

"During all this time of dread and darkness, I virtually stood alone, but remaining true to the dictates of unsullied honor, I steered the infant organization through dangerous channels and finally succeeded in making good. . . ."[10]

At the beginning of 1920 there were but a few chapters scattered throughout the South, most of them in Alabama and Georgia, with a probable total membership well under 2,000. The organized activity of these local Klans up to this time had been quite sporadic. In Mobile, in the summer of 1918, for example, Klansmen as a body spoke out against a shipyard strike and hunted out draft dodgers; in Birmingham, in 1919, they demanded greater police action against the criminal elements of the city; in Atlanta, in 1919, they marched in the parade at the reunion of Confederate Veterans, and at the beginning of the following year met to celebrate the adoption of the Eighteenth (Prohibition) Amendment to the Constitution.

Such slow growth was due in large part to the lack of the right kind of leadership in the highest echelon of authority. Simmons did have faith—he "actually went hungry in order that the bills of the Klan might be met"; he simply did *not* have a head for business enterprise. The Imperial Wizard was, in other words, little more than a dreamer. One who studies the early history of the Klan finds himself readily assenting to the point of view of a well-known contemporary reporter of the order that "had the propagation of the Klan remained in Colonel Simmons' hands, it is fairly certain that the organization would never have attained large dimensions or become a national problem."

The expansion of the Klan began in 1920, the year of its reorganization. On June 7 of that year Simmons, after finally recognizing his limitations, signed a contract with a thoroughly experienced promoter of money drives and a master of publicity, Edward Young Clarke of Atlanta. Before Clarke jonied forces with the "Colonel," he had been at various times a reporter for the *Atlanta Constitution,* a solicitor for the Woodmen of the World (although Simmons had been similarly engaged, the two did not meet until the beginning of 1920), and a worker for the war-fund campaigns of World War I. According to the contract, Simmons was to retain his autocratic control of the Klan but Clarke, as "Imperial Kleagle," was to have a free hand in building up the membership by his own devices.[11] In his role as head of the Propagation Department of the Klan, Clarke found himself relying more and more upon the assistance of his business associate, a plump, fair-haired widow named Mrs. Elizabeth Tyler. It is interesting to note that the latter was not even mentioned in the contract and never held an official post in the Invisible Empire. Let Mrs. Tyler relate how this important, albeit short-lived, triumvirate came to be:

"He [Clarke] was in charge of a great Harvest Festival in Atlanta that brought more people to Atlanta than had ever been there before. I was interested in hygiene work for babies . . . in the Harvest Festival we had a "Better Babies" Parade, of which I had charge. It was through this that I met Mr. Clarke. After we had talked over many business enterprises we formed the Southern Publicity Association

... I financed the Southern Publicity Association and stayed in the office, and Mr. Clarke was field representative.

"We came in contact with Col. Simmons and the Ku Klux Klan through the fact that my son-in-law joined it. We found Col. Simmons was having a hard time to get along ... and he was heart and soul for the success of his Ku Klux Klan. After we had investigated it from every angle, we decided to go into it with Col. Simmons and give it the impetus that it could get best from publicity." [12]

Clarke and Tyler associated themselves with the Klan to make money. In their desire to "sell" the organization, they found it most effective to appeal to the racial, religious, and nationalistic feelings of prospective joiners. Their publicity releases strove to show how the Klan was the country's only bulwark against the evil forces of the Negro, Catholic, Jew, and immigrant. As a direct result of the Clarke-Tyler program the Klan found itself being quickly transformed from a somewhat easy-going southern fraternity of patriotic whites into a violently aggressive national organization of chauvinistic native-born, white Protestants!

In addition to directing publicity with Mrs. Tyler, Clarke, as Imperial Kleagle, attended to the more difficult task of actual recruiting. Under him there was for each Realm of the Invisible Empire a "King Kleagle," to whom in turn there were attached as many "Kleagles" as necessary to do the field work within the Realm. By the middle of 1921 there were over 200 Kleagles active throughout the United States. [13]

The "Klectoken," or $10 fee, collected from each new member was disposed of as follows: the Kleagle kept for himself $4 and remitted $6 to the King Kleagle; the latter retained $1 and sent $5 to the Grand Goblin of the Domain to which he was attached; the Grand Goblin took $.50 and sent $4.50 to the Imperial Kleagle, who in turn kept $2.50 and paid the rest into the coffers of the Imperial Wizard. The entire system was meticulously conducted, with each official required to file his weekly returns.

Clarke and Tyler duly carried out their end of the bargain; within a year and a half after the Southern Publicity Association linked itself with the Klan, the latter grew from a few thousand members to about 100,000.

However, the Imperial Wizard would have one believe that "it wasn't until newspapers began to attack the Klan that it really grew." On September 6, 1921, the *New York World* began a three-week series of bitterly hostile articles on the objectives, methods, and leaders of the Klan. According to this newspaper, the order was merely a group

of avaricious peddlers of bigotry. Eighteen leading newspapers, including such southern journals as the *New Orleans Times-Picayune,*
the *Dallas Morning News,* and the *Columbus, Georgia Enquirer-Sun,*
published the *New York World's* exposure.

The anti-Klan press ultimately had a hand in inducing Congress itself to investigate the order. The House of Representatives Committee
on Rules conducted hearings from October 11 to 17, 1921. Simmons,
on the stand for several days, was ever mindful of the fact that a
defense of the Klan in his own words was being sent by reporters
all over the country. He even sought to "cash in" on this by asserting
that the interest of the House of Representatives Committee on Rules
reflected approval of the Klan.

However unwittingly, the Congressional investigation did give the
secret fraternity a considerable amount of free and valuable advertising.
Upon his return from Washington to national headquarters in Atlanta,[14]
the "Colonel" found himself "literally swamped" with letters from all
parts of the country requesting permission to organize local Klans.
Simmons, Clarke, Tyler, and their respective underlings worked long
hours every day trying to meet the clamorous demand for admittance
into the Invisible Empire—a demand that was to result within the next
year in over 1,100,000 new members. Simmons' observation of all this
was gleeful and succinct: "Congress made us."

The Imperial Wizard soon felt that he needed an energetic, dedicated
man as a personal assistant. After weeks of searching, Clarke finally
found him one—Hiram Wesley Evans. Born in Ashland, Alabama, in
1881, Evans received his formal education at Vanderbilt University in
Nashville, Tennessee, and eventually settled in Dallas, Texas, where
he practiced dentistry. Before he was brought to Atlanta, where
"Colonel" Simmons promptly presented him with the official post of
Kligrapp in his cabinet, Dr. Evans had been the Exalted Cyclops of the
local Klan in Dallas. In his early forties, blue-eyed, round-faced,
pudgy, and genial, Dr. Evans liked to think of himself as "the most
average man in America." But he was no average man; he had within
him both the deep faith of Simmons and the vast practicality of
Clarke.

In March, 1922, upon the insistence of his wife, who feared that he
was on the verge of a nervous collapse, Simmons took a six months'
leave of absence from his Klan duties, during which time Clarke
served as Imperial Wizard *ad interim.* Upon returning, restored neither
in strength nor spirit, yet shuddering at the thought of relinquishing
the great office he held, the "Colonel" evolved a plan whereby he

could have his cake and eat it too. He decided to summon a Klonvoka-tion so that it could, during the course of its business, re-elect him as Imperial Wizard and provide him with a coadjutor who could relieve him of the many and varied petty details of planning and implementing policy. He suggested that this new administrative assistant be called "Emperor."

The Klonvokation was called for November 27, 1922, in Atlanta. At about four o'clock that morning Simmons was roused from his sleep by two agitated Klansmen: David Curtis Stephenson and Fred L. Savage. The former was a coal dealer from Indianapolis who as Grand Dragon of the Realm of Indiana had acquired both immense wealth and great power in the politics of his state. The latter was an ex-New York City pier detective who as "Imperial Night Hawk" in Sim-mons' cabinet was the head of the Klan secret service with a force of fifty or so special agents.

As "Colonel" Simmons later told it, the following conversation took place:

"Mr. Savage became grave and very pointedly said, 'Don't you permit your name to come before the Klonvokation for nomination as Imperial Wizard ... We have the information that if your name is men-tioned on the floor of the Klonvokation, there are men there who are going to get up and attack your character ... I have got men placed and have given orders to shoot and shoot to kill any ... man that attacks the character of Colonel Simmons. Consequently, a rough house is going to be provoked and the Klonvokation will be destroyed. Now in order to preserve the harmony and the peace and the wonder-ful carrying on of the Klonvokation as we have it, let us beat those birds and you give them a message in which you refuse to allow your name to come before them to succeed yourself.

"After a few minutes' pause they ... asked me if I wouldn't name as my choice Hiram Wesley Evans, in order to meet the situation. I told them ... that there was nothing on the board against Hiram Wesley Evans and that he might fit in an emergency as he had know-ledge of the workings of the office, has been there a year with it.

"They said, 'Then you name Dr. Evans as your successor?' I said, 'Under the circumstances and facts of this little conference here, I am agreeable to him.' "[15]

The Klonvokation elected Dr. Evans as Imperial Wizard and in-stalled "Colonel" Simmons as Emperor, after redrafting the constitution to provide for the new office.

Then Simmons learned that the early morning visit from the Grand

Dragon of the Realm of Indiana and the Imperial Night Hawk was but an integral part of a *coup d'état* engineered by these two men with the assistance of H. C. McCall, a former constable of Houston and a leader of the Klan there, and James A. Comer, Grand Dragon of the Realm of Arkansas. Simmons found out that many hours before Stephenson and Savage awakened him that morning they had sent a handful of henchmen to the hotel rooms of the various influential members of the Klonvokation to convince them that the Imperial Wizardship should go to Evans.

It should be noted that after the Klonvokation Evans asserted that he had no knowledge of the intrigue in which "the boys" had engaged in his behalf, that his elevation to the highest office in the Klan had been a complete and total surprise. Simmons was never able to believe this.

Concomitant with the election of Evans to the Imperial Wizardship was the disruption of the triumvirate of Simmons, Clarke, and Tyler. At the beginning of 1923 Mrs. Tyler married an affluent Atlanta movie theater proprietor and so left active Klan work to take up once more the chores of a household. The following year she died. Just as soon as Evans found it propitious, he cancelled Clarke's contract as organizer. On March 5, 1923, an announcement came from the Imperial Aulic that Clarke had been removed "for the good of the order" and would no longer receive "one cent of revenue from the Klan." By the late spring of 1923 Evans had accomplished the transfer of all the significant duties of the Emperorship to the Imperial Wizardship; "Colonel" Simmons, by now a semi-invalid, was stripped of even those last remaining bits of power that he had enjoyed after the *coup d'état*. On May 1-2, 1923, at a special meeting of the Kloncilium, the Ku Klux Klan bought from Simmons various copyrights to the organization, in return for which it agreed to pay him $1,000 a month for the rest of his life. The following September Simmons resigned from the Klan and relinquished all legal interests in the order for a flat sum of $146,500. The "Colonel" remained for many years in Atlanta, where he made several attempts to organize orders similar to the Klan. He finally gave up in despair, and left for Luverne, Alabama, where he ended his days in quiet retirement. In 1945 he died.

While Evans was the undisputed ruler of the Knights of the Ku Klux Klan he made certain changes which he looked upon as reforms. First, each functionary was given a moderate salary instead of receiving, as heretofore, large sums out of receipts from initiation fees and the sale of regalia.[16] Second, any Klansman of questionable morals was expelled from the organization, and the private life of the applicant for membership was now quite closely scrutinized. Third, any act of terrorism engaged in by Klansmen was vigorously denounced; in order to curtail lawless activities of members hiding behind Klan regalia, the wearing of the hood and robe was forbidden except at formal ceremonies.[17] Fourth, from a "band of twentieth century knights, without fear and without reproach," the order was molded into a powerful force in the local, state, and national politics of America.

Evans' "reform" policy could not eradicate the widespread antipathy toward the Klan which had been incurred during the heyday of the Simmons-Clarke-Tyler regime. The public still remained incensed at the accumulation of riches by the former hierarchy of the secret fraternity.[18] As Imperial Wizard, Simmons had enjoyed a salary of $1,000 a month and unlimited personal and official expense accounts. Among the many gifts from his followers there had been a $33,000 home in Atlanta known as "Klankrest," two high-priced automobiles, and an appropriation of $25,000 as compensation for those early years of unremunerative service to the Invisible Empire.[19] From just after the Congressional investigation of the Klan in October, 1921, until his expulsion from the order in March, 1923, Clarke, as Imperial Kleagle, had received as much as $40,000 a month. Stephenson had owned a lavishly furnished mansion in a suburb of Indianapolis, a costly yacht on Lake Michigan, a private railroad car, and a gilded airplane (complete with personal pilot). All in all, this Grand Dragon of the Realm of Indiana had amassed from his office a fortune of $3,000,000.

America was still disgusted by the scandalous private lives of former high-ranking Klansmen. As years had passed, Simmons had become a near-drunkard.[20] It is not unlikely that the "Colonel's" inveterate drinking was a factor in the nervous illness he had suffered just before losing the Imperial Wizardship. In October, 1919, in Atlanta, Clarke and Mrs. Tyler had been arrested together and fined for disorderly conduct; that is, for having been intoxicated and not fully clad. The arrest had taken place on information given by Clarke's wife, who had a fortnight previously sued for divorce on the ground of desertion. In September, 1923, Clarke had been placed under bond for carrying whiskey in his traveling bag. In November, 1924, the U. S. federal court at Houston had found Clarke guilty and fined him $5,000 for having violated the White Slave Act in February, 1921.[21] Every time Stephenson had given a party—and he had been famous for them—he had loaded his mansion with wine and women to insure hours of fun for the many guests. Stephenson himself had liked the

ladies. One to whom he had given much attention (years after desert-
ing first one, then another, wife) was an employee of the Indiana
Department of Public Welfare, Miss Madge Oberholtzer. In March,
1925, after having had sadistic sexual relations forced upon her by
Stephenson, Miss Oberholtzer had written an anguished note and
swallowed a fatal dose of poison. After a trial that had attracted widespread attention, Stephenson had been found guilty of murder and
sentenced to life imprisonment.[22]

The nation could not forget the past activities of the Klansmen who
had looked upon their organization as a nationwide vigilance committee. These self-appointed protectors of a community's morals and
peace had taken such measures against wrongdoers (either real or
imagined) as ostracism, boycotting, the sending of threatening letters
and even "night-riding," the culmination of which was tar and feathering, whipping, branding, or emasculation. As a matter of fact Evans'
effort to discourage the maltreating of erring citizens by Klansmen
was less than successful.

If the first three of Evans' "reforms" did not assuage the nation's
wrath toward the Klan, the fourth served only to augment that wrath.
The public became chafed at a fraternal organization which more
and more demanded the right and oftener and oftener was able to
"express itself" in the political field.

This "reform" policy of Evans' could never have eradicated the widespread antipathy toward the Klan because the order remained, in
essence, what it had long been—a champion of native-born, white
Protestantism. As such, the secret fraternity under Evans—as under
Simmons, Clarke, and Tyler—automatically made enemies of large
numbers of Americans—anyone who happened to be foreign-born,
Negro, Catholic, Jewish, or opposed to bigotry and chauvinism.[23]

As the third decade of the twentieth century approached a close,
the Knights of the Ku Klux Klan was no longer able to maintain its
membership. In 1924, there had been more than 4,000,000 members.
By 1926 the membership had shrunk to fewer than 1,500,000. By
1928 it had shriveled to about 200,000. In 1928, however, the Klan
spirit, if not the Klan organized political potency of former years, was
a factor in cracking the "Solid South," when the Democratic party's
candidate for the presidency was a Catholic, Alfred E. Smith. Then,
what was left of the Invisible Empire collapsed. By 1930 its membership had withered away to scarcely 50,000. And with the depression
of this new decade, the secret order was all but forgotten.[24]

Chapter II

EXPANSION IN THE 1920'S

It is a serious mistake to think that the Ku Klux Klan of the 1920's was a powerful force only in the Deep South. To be sure, the order was founded in Georgia, and then spread rather quickly to the neighboring states of Alabama and Florida. However, the Klan reached its first peak of success, after the Congressional investigation in October, 1921, in the vast area to the west of the lower Mississippi River, in Texas, Oklahoma, and Arkansas. Then the organization took firm root on the Pacific coast, first in California and later in Oregon. And by 1924 the fraternity reached extraordinary success in the Middle West generally and fantastic success in the states of Indiana and Ohio particularly.[1]

One of the most astute of the many contemporary students of the Klan, Stanley Frost, calculated that the order at its height of activity had about 4,000,000 members distributed as follows: Indiana, 500,000; Ohio, 450,000; Texas, 415,000; California, New York, Oklahoma, Oregon 200,000 each; Alabama, Arkansas, Florida, Georgia, Illinois, Kansas, Kentucky, Louisiana, Maryland, Michigan, Mississippi, Missouri, New Jersey, Tennessee, Washington, and West Virginia, between 50,000 and 200,000 each.

One might wonder at the large number of Klansmen in states having so few Negroes, Catholics, Jews, or foreign-born—states lacking, therefore, in all those things against which the Klan railed and upon which it thrived. The secret is that in the 1920's the bulk of the people in the states of the western reaches of the lower Mississippi Valley, the Pacific coast, and the Middle West were the descendants—both physical and spiritual—of that old American stock from which the anti-Catholic and nativistic movements of the preceding century drew their chief support.

The Klan was in the main a village and small town phenomenon. Neither the city, as a potpourri of many racial, religious, and ethnic groups, nor the country, as an isolated area with far-spread inhabitants, lent itself to the effective launching and developing of a local chapter. The appreciable Klan following in many of the large cities and much of the countryside all over the United States during the 1920's must not be discounted. But the secret fraternity drew its millions primarily from the villages and small towns which had been left rather undisturbed by the immigration, industrialization, and liberal thought of modern America.

Eligible for membership in the Invisible Empire, Knights of the Ku Klux Klan was any white, native-born, Christian, American male, who (in order to debar Catholics) owed "no allegiance of any nature or degree to any foreign government, nation, institution, sect, ruler, person . . ."[2]

Among those millions of individuals who could, and did, join the order, one contemporary observer, Robert L. Duffus, found six classes: (1) the organizers and promoters; (2) businessmen; (3) politicians; (4) preachers and pious laymen; (5) incorrigible "joiners" and lovers of "horseplay"; and (6) bootleggers who joined for protection. Using this classification as the basis for a discussion of the caliber of men who associated themselves with the Klan—and this classification will have to serve for lack of another by a contemporary more knowledgeable and objective—it becomes immediately apparent that Klansmen belonged to a variety of socio-economic classes.

Not always, but sometimes, the leaders of a community would join the local Klan chapter. In each new territory that the Kleagle "worked," he made a practice, for obvious reasons, of approaching the prominent citizens first. Imperial Kligrapp H. K. Ramsey, writing of the Klan's Second Klonvokation, held in Kansas City, Missouri, in September, 1924, declared that "Ministers of the Gospel, Attorneys (some representing our common judiciary), Educators, business men (a number of them millionaires and capitalists) . . . all sat together."

After the Kleagles had flattered and persuaded as many of the leading citizens of the community into joining the secret fraternity as they could, they then turned their attention to enlisting the middle class. The remark of Ramsey, as a member of the Klan's hierarchy, might well be taken with the proverbial grain of salt. Nevertheless, it is most important to note that practically all anti-Klan writers described the vast majority of Klansmen as members of America's respectable middle class. One journalist, for example, wrote that most Klansmen were "solid, respectable citizens, kind and loving husbands and fathers, conscientious members of their churches"; another penned that most of the persons who joined the order were "good, solid, middle-class citizens, the 'backbone of the Nation'."

After the Kleagles had enlisted as many of the middle class as they were able, they then directed their sales talk to the less desirable elements. Hustling agents "sought out the poor, the romantic, the short-witted, the bored, the vindictive, the bigoted, and the ambitious, and sold them their heart's desire." Stanley Frost, in his reportorial study of the Klan for *The Outlook,* commented that he had not learned of a single case in which a Kleagle refused an individual membership in the secret fraternity—"no matter how vicious or dangerous he might be"—if he had the necessary $10. Henry Peck Fry, who resigned from the Klan as a disillusioned Kleagle, branded his former colleagues for "selling memberships as they would sell insurance or stock."

It was this indiscriminate recruiting by Kleagles (resulting, naturally, from the fact that their incomes depended upon the number of men enlisted) that forced one W. M. Likins to sever all contacts with his local Klan chapter. This individual joined the secret fraternity because he believed in its nationalistic and Protestant creed; he soon quit the organization because he found it to contain an element of "low characters, not educated or moral." Most chapters had their share of the community's dregs on their membership lists. In the South this element seemed to be an active minority in most localities, and a forceful majority in some.

There was something about the United States of the 1920's that influenced a surprisingly large number of Americans in their decision to join the order. The spirit of the times demands analysis.

The decade 1920-1930 was what it was largely because of the effects of World War I. During the armed struggle America mistrusted and mistreated aliens, deprived itself of food and fuel, and poured its money into the Liberty Loan campaigns. But the war was over too quickly for the nation to spend fully its ultra-patriotic psychological feelings. In the decade following, America permitted itself to reject the League of Nations, to curtail immigration, to deport aliens wholesale, and to accept the Klan with its motto of "one hundred per cent Americanism."

Another result of the war was the intensifying of racial antipathies. The bearing of arms and the freedom of contact with whites in France by Negro servicemen and the receiving of high wages by many Negroes of the South who moved to northern cities in order to work for war industries made the colored people of the nation feel a human dignity they had never before experienced. During the 1920's this served to increase hostility on the part of whites and to decrease the endurance of such hostility on the part of Negroes. The Klan was quick to capitalize on the feeling of those whites who believed they saw everywhere Negro "uppitiness."

A third effect of World War I was the violent death of the old American way of life—evangelical, didactic, prudish—and the sudden birth of a new. (No event serves as a nation's cultural watershed better than a war.) The 1920's meant "modernism." And "modernism," among other things, meant the waning of church influence, particularly over the younger people; the breaking down of parental control; the discarding of the old-fashioned absolute moral code in favor of a freer or "looser" personal one, which manifested itself in such activities as purchasing and drinking contraband liquor, participating in ultra-frank conversations between the sexes, wearing skirts close to the knees, engaging in various extreme forms of dancing in smoke-filled road houses, and petting in parked cars. A host of Americans were unwilling, or unable, to adapt themselves to this post-war culture. In the Klan they saw a bulwark against the hated "modernism," an opportunity to salvage some of the customs and traditions of the old religio-moralistic order.

Although there was a spirit peculiar to the 1920's that influenced many into joining the secret fraternity, each individual had his own particular reason for donning the peaked hood and robe. Why certain leading citizens of a community were prompted to associate themselves with the Klan is not difficult to comprehend. Many businessmen most assuredly saw that by joining the Klan they could keep old and get new trade through their fraternal contacts; some physicians and lawyers must have realized that as the "best" of their community they would probably be the officers of the local chapter of the ever-growing order; numerous Protestant clergymen were undoubtedly won over by the organization's highly moral and religious ritual and code;[3] large numbers of local politicians were ever mindful of the fact that each fellow Klansman would equal one vote they could count on.

Droves of middle-class Southerners eagerly paid the $10 initiation fee to the first Kleagle with whom they came in contact. Southern history had idealized the old Klan as a protector of the "peculiar way of life" below the Mason-Dixon line to the extent that to many inhabitants of that area the memory of the Reconstruction organization was something sacred. Besides, there was in the 1920's a new, vibrant interest in the old hooded order, for David W. Griffith's cinematic eulogy on the Klan, "The Birth of a Nation," had been thrilling the movie-going public since its first release in 1915. There was hardly a southern city that had not had the film for a return engagement.[4] Thus when the twentieth century Klan was presented to the people as a memorial to the old organization, half the battle for recruitment in the South had been won.

That the bigoted of the nation found "truth" in the Klan is self-evident. It must be emphasized that the secret order was most shrewd in the way it varied its appeal from one section of the country to the other to suit the paramount prejudice of the area. The Klan's plank was chameleonic: on the Pacific coast it was anti-Japanese; in the Southwest, anti-Mexican; in the Middle West, anti-Catholic;[5] in the Deep South, anti-Negro; in New England, anti-French Canadian; in the large cities of the Northeast, anti-alien-born; on the Atlantic coast, anti-Semitic.

Many ruffians took the sacred oath of allegiance to the Invisible Empire. The Klan as a bulwark against "modernism" conveyed to the simple and sincere members of the order nothing more than a crusade to reform the wayward of their community. Translated into practical application such a crusade meant teaching someone a "lesson" —perhaps an adulterous neighbor, the town drunkard, a merchant who habitually short-changed and short-weighted, or a corrupt official. Taking punitive measures against a wrongdoer without benefit of the regularly established police and court systems leads more often than not to injustice and cruelty. While appearing to be acting selflessly in behalf of the Klan, hoodlums saw a wonderful opportunity to get their fill of sadistic orgies. Taking refuge under the hood and robe, rowdies on a "night-riding" mission could wield with abandon the tar bucket and bag of feathers, whip, branding iron, acid bottle, or pocket knife.[6]

Why the bored, the romantic, the fraternally inclined, and the lovers of "horseplay" joined the Klan is obvious. The world of the Invisible Empire was a world of make-believe. One critic of the order, Aldrich Blake, put it nicely: "When a man joins the Ku Klux Klan, a sensation seems to come over him as definite as falling in love. He simply drops out of society and enters a new world." During the day a man was a breadwinner, going through an ofttimes dull, always tiring, routine at the office or shop. But after dark a man became a Knight, taking part in activities that were pure spectacle and mystery, fun and excitement. How satisfying it must have been to many to have been able to participate, for example, in a ritual-packed business meeting in a room decked out with an altar full of symbolic objects and illuminated by a "fiery cross," or in an initiation ceremony long after midnight in a lonely wood outside of town.

Then there was the costume. The robe of the rank and file of the secret order was of white cotton, girdled with a sash of the same color and material, and with a white cross upon a red background stitched below the left shoulder. The headdress was a white cotton peaked hood from which a red tassel hung. The entire outfit cost $5. The costume of an officer was more resplendent and more expensive, how much so depending upon the status of the officer in the Klan hierarchy. The robe of a Grand Dragon, for example, was of orange satin trimmed with military braid and embroidered in silk. Together with an orange satin peaked hood, it cost $40.[7]

There were parades. These were usually night affairs, held rather often by most local Klans of the villages and small towns, and only on very special occasions by those of the cities. Men, women, and children from near and far would gather on the sidewalks of the main thoroughfare of a hamlet to gaze upon the hooded and robed men, beneath burning torches and behind a huge fiery cross, filing silently down the street. A mayor from Texas, in describing the reaction of the thousands of people who were witnessing a Klan parade in his small town, avowed that throughout the entire demonstration, one could almost hear the breathing of the crowd.[8]

A "Kalendar" was used. The fixed point in time employed for computing the years of this calendar was 1867, when there was effected in Nashville, Tennessee, a general organization of the many local post-Civil War Klans. In the Kalendar the seven days of the week were, in order, "dark, deadly, dismal, doleful, desolate, dreadful, and desperate"; the five weeks of the month were "woeful, weeping, wailing, wonderful, and weird"; the twelve months of the year were "bloody, gloomy, hideous, fearful, furious, alarming, terrible, horrible, mournful, sorrowful, frightful, and appalling." Thus the date of the proclamation of the revised Klan constitution, November 29, 1922, was "the Doleful Day of the Weird Week of the Frightful Month of the Year of the Klan LVI."

There was even "Klonversation." A typical verbal encounter:

"Ayak?" (Are you a Klansman?)

"Akia." (A Klansman I am.)

"Cyknar." (Call your Klan number and Realm.)

"No.1, Atga." (Number 1 Klan of Atlanta, Georgia.)

"Kigy." (Klansman, I greet you.)

"Sanbog." (Strangers are near. Be on guard.)

Various emblems and tokens could be purchased. Any member of the order was able to obtain a "Kluxer's Knifty Knife" for $1.25, a bargain indeed, considering the fact that the little instrument was a "real 100 per cent knife for 100 per cent Americans." If a Klansman wanted to surprise his spouse, he might get her, for only $2.25, a zircon-studded Fiery Cross, which was outfitted with a clasp so that it could be worn as a brooch. The larger-sized Fiery Cross, costing $2.90, had a link at the top so that a Knight could wear it on the watch chain across his vest. Five dollars purchased one a fourteen karat gold-filled ring with a ten karat solid gold Klan emblem on a fiery red stone.

Naturally, it was expected of every individual who took the sacred oath of allegiance to the Invisible Empire, Knights of the Ku Klux Klan to know and fully accept the beliefs of the order. The main tenets in the creed of the secret fraternity were the following: (1) memorialization of the original Klan; (2) white supremacy; (3) anti-Semitism; (4) anti-foreign-bornism; (5) anti-Catholicism; (6) "pure" Americanism; (7) Protestantism and strict morality.

Although the twentieth century Klan came to possess a more complex ideology than the Reconstruction Klan, at its founding and for the first five years of its existence its *raison d'être* was the memorialization of its nineteenth century namesake. Even after the Klan had been transformed from a southern fraternity of a few thousand into a national organization with millions of members, its leaders were quick to bring to mind that the order was the proud heir of the original Klan. In 1922, while serving as Imperial Wizard *ad interim,* Clarke declared, "By right of our sacred inheritance, we glory in wearing the regalia of the original Ku Klux Klan as a memorial to that dauntless organization of the Reconstruction Days." The following year "Colonel" Simmons in one of his books wrote, "The present Klan is a memorial to the original organization. In a sense it is the reincarnation among the sons of the spirit of the fathers."

The twentieth century Klan copied a great deal from its precursor— the hierarchy of officers, subdivisional structure, regalia, silent parades, and mysterious language. There was only one thing, however, taken over from the original Klan by the twentieth century order which was ideological in nature rather than ritualistic or ornamental—and that was the belief in white supremacy.[9]

A quick and highly satisfactory method by which to approach the Klan's thinking on the Negro (as well as on such topics as the Jew, foreign-born, Catholic, or Americanism) is to dip into a few of the writings of, addresses by, and interviews with Evans, for as Imperial Wizard he spoke officially for every man in the order. In an article for *The North American Review,* Evans declared:

"The world has been so made that each race must fight for its

life, must conquer, accept slavery or die. The Klansman believes that
the whites will not become slaves, and he does not intend to die before
his time.

"... the future of progress and civilization depends on the continual supremacy of the white race. The forward movement of the
world for centuries has come entirely from it. Other races each had
its chance and either failed or stuck fast, while white civilization
shows no sign of having reached its limit. Until the whites falter,
or some colored civilization has a miracle of awakening, there is not a
single colored stock that can claim even equality with the white; much
less supremacy."

Fully satisfied that centuries of history had proved the basic infer-
iority of the colored people all over the world, Evans felt compelled, in
a speech given in Dallas, Texas, on October 24, 1923, before 75,000
Klansmen, to debar from American nationality the Negroes: "They
have not, they can not, attain the Anglo-Saxon level ... The low men-
tality of savage ancestors, of jungle environment, is inherent in
the blood-stream of the colored race in America. No new environment can more than superficially overcome this age-old hereditary
handicap."

But the Klan believed that America must act kindly and helpfully
toward its Negro inhabitants, Evans told an interviewer, for while
"America must face the fact that God Almighty never intended social
equality for Negro and white man," she "owes it to the Negro to give
him every privilege and protection and every opportunity consistent
with ... National safety."

In a pamphlet much circulated by the Invisible Empire in 1923,
Ideals of the Ku Klux Klan, there appears a section entitled "Character
of the Organization," containing the following list:

"1. This is a white man's organization.
2. This is a gentile organization.
3. It is an American organization.
4. It is a Protestant organization."[10]

Just as Evans pleaded the Klan's cause for white supremacy, he
explained feelingly on behalf of his fraternal followers why the order
was also a "gentile," "American," and "Protestant" one, striving to
make Protestantism and native-bornism prerequisites for American
nationality.[11]

During an extended conversation with a journalist, Evans said that
the reason the Klan was antipathetic toward the Jew was that "for two
thousand years [he] has rigidly adhered to a racial limitation of inter-

marriage which makes it impossible for him to be assimilated into American life wholly and unreservedly." At another time, however, the Imperial Wizard attempted to show that the Jew was unassimilable for reasons other than a disinclination to marry outside his faith: "By every patriotic test, he is an alien and unassimilable. Not in a thousand years of continuous residence would he form basic attachments comparable to those the older type of immigrant would form within a year. The evil influence of persecutions is upon him. It is as tho he was here today and might be forced to flee tomorrow. He does not tie himself to the land."

But Evans, along with the Klan of course, grew gradually to consider the Jew a far smaller problem than other "unassimilables" in the nation: "For one thing, he is confined to a few cities, and is no problem at all to most of the country. For another thing, his exclusiveness, political activities, and refusal to become assimilated are racial rather than religious, based on centuries of persecution. They cannot last long in the atmosphere of free America, and we may expect that with the passage of time the serious aspects of this problem will fade away."

The very heart of the Klan's thinking on the foreign-born in America can be found in a single passage from one of Evans' articles for *The Forum*:

"We believe that the pioneers who built America bequeathed to their own children a priority right to it, the control of it and of its future, and that no one on earth can claim any part of this inheritance except through our generosity. We believe, too, that the mission of America under Almighty God is to perpetuate and develop just the kind of nation and just the kind of civilization which our forefathers created... Also, we believe... that the American stock, which was bred under highly selective surroundings, has proved its value and should not be [through intermarriage with the foreign-born] mongrelized... Finally, we believe that all foreigners were admitted with the idea, and on the basis of at least an implied understanding, that they would ... adopt our ideas and ideals, and help in fulfilling our destiny along those lines, but never that they should be permitted to force us to change into anything else."

To the Klansman the foreign-born "problem" readily brought to mind two other questions, universal suffrage and immigration. Regarding the former, the Klan was convinced that there must be a "restricting [of] the franchise to men and women who are able through birth and education to understand Americanism... [which]

means practically a restriction to native-born children who have had the benefit of the training given by the American educational system ..." As to immigration, "since American thought and life have been and are being prevented from their true course by excessive alien mixture," the secret order believed in "an immediate complete stoppage of immigration; the stoppage to remain complete until reason appears for again accepting foreign immigration."

In the Dallas speech of October 24, 1923, in which he declared Negroes unworthy of American nationality, Evans described Catholics as forming an element "whose assimilation is impossible without the gravest danger to our institutions," since "no nation can long endure that permits a higher temporal allegiance than to its own government."

Regarding Roman Catholic clerics, the Imperial Wizard had something special to say about their being incapable, because of religious hindrance, of attaining the "100 per cent American standard": "To them the Presidency at Washington is subordinate to the priesthood in Rome. The parochial school alone is sufficient proof of a divided allegiance, a separatist instinct. They demand that our future citizens be trained not in public schools but under the control and influence of a priesthood that teaches supreme loyalty to a religious oligarchy that is not even of American domicile."

But the Klan's anti-Catholicism stemmed not quite so much from an ignorance of Catholic dogma and ritual or the intentions of the Catholic priesthood as it did from the belief that the Catholic Church already controlled the votes of most of its communicants, and was seeking to regain fully the vast political power it had in centuries past. Evans said, "The real objection to Romanism in America is not that it is a religion,—which is no objection at all,—but that it is a church in politics; an organized, disciplined, powerful rival to every political government. A religion in politics is serious; a church in politics is deadly to free institutions."

The Klan had a great deal to say about the "pure" Americanism which it maintained was forever beyond the grasp of Negroes, Jews, the foreign-born, and Catholics. Ever ready was the secret fraternity to define Americanism, and to show the very special affinity its members possessed for this phenomenon, and to offer counsel on how a loyal attachment to the United States might be preserved, and even developed.

Acclaimed by his fellow Knights as "about the most 100 per cent American of all the 100 per cent Americans in the United States,"

Evans surely felt confident of their support when he wrote the following passage about the character of this intangible force, Americanism, "It has, to be sure, certain defined principles . . . Democracy is one, fair dealing, impartial justice, equal opportunity, religious liberty, independence, self-reliance, courage, endurance, acceptance of individual responsibility as well as individual rewards for effort, willingness to sacrifice for the good of his family, his nation and his race before anything else but God, dependence on enlightened conscience for guidance, the right to unhampered development—these are fundamental."

Concerning the relationship of Knights to Americanism, two choice bits from Evans' extended remarks on the subject will give a broad hint of official Klan thinking: "The Klan is an organization to promote practical patriotism—Americanism. Its ideal is to restore and then to preserve and develop the old, fundamental ideas on which the Nation was founded and which have made it great . . ."; "He [the Klansman] believes religiously that a betrayal of Americanism . . . is treason to the most sacred of trusts, a trust from his fathers and a trust from God."

The Klan believed that only through a public educational system which stressed the "value and beauty of true citizenship" could a mighty and vibrant America be created. Therefore, the order swore to fight for the extension of the public school system all over the nation, in spite of the continuous refusal of certain bodies, such as the Catholic Church, to give up their own private educational programs.

The Klan's interest in education, however, went deeper than a concern for the protection of the public elementary and secondary school system. As a matter of fact, the order felt so strongly about education for the preservation of Americanism that it made two separate attempts to set up a Klan college, the first during Simmons' Imperial Wizardship and the second during Evans'. In August, 1921, the Klan acquired Lanier University in Atlanta, the Baptist institution where Simmons had once been an instructor in Southern history. Co-educational, and open to the children of native-born, white Protestants only, the new school dedicated itself to the teaching of "pure, 100 per cent Americanism." Failing to gain an adequate enrollment, the Klan gave up this academic enterprise, only to negotiate, two years later, for the taking over of Valparaiso University in Valparaiso, Indiana. In this instance, however, all attempts to acquire the institution met with failure.

The Klan cherished a belief in Protestant Christian doctrine. Although it did not require an applicant to hold church membership, it did insist upon his embracing the tenets of Protestantism. The Klan endorsed no one religious denomination. Many Knights, however, were adherents to "the old-time religion," with its faith in the Bible as the literal and unalterable word of God. So many Klansmen (especially those of the South) belonged to the evangelical sects that the public came to think that one of the articles of faith of the Klan was Fundamentalism.[12]

Succinct expression of the official religious beliefs of the secret fraternity was once given by Imperial Klokard William James Mahoney:

"We magnify the Bible—as the basis of our Constitution, the foundation of our government, the source of our laws, the sheet-anchor of our liberties, the most practical guide of right living, and the source of all true wisdom.

"We teach the worship of God.

"We honor the Christ, as the Klansman's only *criterion of character.* And we seek at His hands that cleansing from sin and impurity, which only He can give.

"We believe that the highest expression of life is in service and in sacrifice for that which is right . . . . [and that] a Klansman must be moved by unselfish motives, such as characterized our Lord the Christ, and moved Him to the highest service and the supreme sacrifice for that which was right."

Religion and morals go hand in hand. If the order was interested in matters of religion, it was preoccupied with the question of morals. Consider, for example, a broadside sent out by the Klan in Indiana. Taking into account the propaganda-recruitment purpose for which the handbill was intended, and disregarding its anti-Catholic portions, one easily gathers from the printed sheet that the Invisible Empire regarded itself as a mighty bulwark of a proper code of morals. "Remember," the handbill read:

"Every criminal, every gambler, every thug, every libertine, every girl ruiner, every home wrecker, every wife beater, every dope peddler, every moonshiner, every crooked politician, every pagan Papist priest, every shyster lawyer, every K. of C., every white slaver, every brothel madam, every Rome controlled newspaper, every black spider—is fighting the Klan. Think it over. Which side are you on?"

In one issue of perhaps the most outspoken pro-Klan newspaper in the entire nation, the *Houston Colonel Mayfield's Weekly,* editor Billie Mayfield spelled out for his readers the specifics of the order's moral crusade:

"It is going to drive the bootleggers forever out of this land and place whiskey-making on a parity with counterfeiting.

"It is going to bring clean moving pictures to this country; it is going to bring clean literature to this country ... It is going to break up roadside parking, and see that the young man who induces a young girl to get drunk is held accountable. It is going to enforce the laws of this land; it is going to protect homes ... The Klan means a new era in the life of America. It means the return of old time Southern chivalry and deference to womanhood; it means that the 'married man with an affinity' has no place in our midst."

Noticeable about the preceding articles of faith of the Klan is their defensive nature. The secret fraternity aimed to preserve, protect, and prevent. The methods used to carry out this regulative program (in addition to the common propaganda techniques so many organizations employ) might be reduced to the following: (1) "Klannishness"; (2) charitable enterprise; (3) "meddling" and terrorism; (4) political activity.

Of all the methods employed by the Klan to carry out its regulative program, the one used most frequently by the membership was the practicing of Klannishness. To an inhabitant of the Invisible Empire Klannishness meant, basically, two things: protecting the reputation, physical being, and business interests of a Klansman and his family; and defending America's flag, Constitution, laws and mores.

Imperial Wizard Evans once described the various facets of Klannishness. According to him, there were three separate aspects of a Klansman's relationship to his confreres—social, moral, and vocational. Regarding vocational Klannishness he wrote, "Patronize Klan business, turn profits to Klansmen if possible. 'You must not tell this person why you insist on him seeing this particular real estate man, other than that he is worthy and deals honorably. He is a Klansman and you can safely recommend him.'"

It is only natural for a fraternal organization to encourage business intercourse among its members. The practical application of the positive philosophy of vocational Klannishness, however, came to mean the very negative practice of boycotting. Knights were never ordered to stop trading with a particular businessman; they were simply given information to show that the individual in question was, for one reason or another, an undesirable member of the community. Free either to act or not on such information, all Klansmen seem to have chosen the former course. To illustrate, at a meeting of a local Klan in a town in northern Ohio, one of the officers made the following remarks:

"I wish to tell you some of the things your fellow-townsmen have done. The Elite Clothing Store sells half-cotton goods as pure wool. Arthur Fredericks, a doctor, is a dope user. John Polaris, a restaurant-keeper, has been trafficking in women. Michael O'Flynn's soft-drink parlor sells white mule. Walter Peters got a slice of that paving contract graft. Jim Brady, the cigar-store man, has a starving wife in Omaha and has been making love to some girls here. Benjamin Strauss, the dry-goods man, underpays his girls, and besides expects too much from them—you understand. Fred Preston's drugstore will give you the white stuff if you know the sign. John Barton joined the Klan just to get trade, and has been turned out."

The speech, noteworthy for its comprehensiveness and lack (on the surface, at least) of racial or religious antipathy, contained no recommendation for a course of action on the part of the audience. Klansmen in that town, however, took much pride in the fact that over a period of time sixty business establishments had fully succumbed to their boycotting measures.

In the eyes of the public, a much less defensible boycotting which developed out of the practice of vocational Klannishness was the shunning of business concerns simply because the proprietor or his help was Negro, Catholic, Jewish, or foreign-born. The Klan, it is interesting to note, was once actually induced by a virulently anti-Catholic organization to boycott a famous brand of cigarettes, Camels, because they were manufactured by a concern said to have been controlled by a well-known Catholic capitalist, Thomas Fortune Ryan.

Of all the activities of the Invisible Empire, the one which was least open to attack by critics of the Klan was its participation in charitable enterprises. Members of the order were commanded to act collectively to "relieve the injured and the opressed; to succor the suffering and unfortunate, especially widows and orphans." Although the national body rarely conducted a charity campaign of its own, and the local chapter generally did not participate in the organized drives conducted by the community to which it belonged, the latter often gave a great deal of aid to the individually needy. It was usual for the chapter to have a special committee which would investigate requests for charity. The recipients of all Klan benevolence were native-born, white Protestants, and the families of members were given preference.[18]

A most common form of Klan almsgiving was the aiding of a minister and his congregation. Customarily, a handful of Klansmen, decked out in full regalia, would enter a church during services, advance silently toward the pulpit, present the pastor with an envelope containing money, and then file out quickly and quietly. On Palm Sunday, 1922, at the Westminster Presbyterian Church in Sacramento, California, for example:

"... six supposed members of the mystic order appeared with the suddenness of an apparition ... shortly after the close of the evening sermon, marched to the altar with the precision of a military drill squad, and handed the Rev. William E. Harrison, the pastor, a sealed envelope, which contained a new $50 bank note and a typewritten letter explaining the gift and commending the work of the minister.

"Moving in unison they left as quickly as they came, never uttering a sound. . . . No one could be found . . . who saw them approach the church or who witnessed their departure or the means of their conveyance. . . ."

A congregation that might have been displeased at having its services interrupted by hooded and robed figures was usually too startled to do anything but accept the gift docilely. There is one instance on record, however, of an unheralded visit by Klansmen which ended with their being routed by a particularly husky and irate usher.

Of all the practices of Klansmen, the one most often and vehemently criticized was the taking of a meddling or terroristic course of action in an attempt to prescribe personal conduct. It appears that each local Klan decided its chief task was the regulation of the morals of the community in which it existed. A typical chapter operated something like this: every Knight considered himself a dectective whose duty it was to go about the community spying on the morals of his fellow residents, the objects of the surveillance being entirely unaware of it, as only Klansmen knew who the members of the order were. When the chapter met, every Knight reported the information he had collected on his neighbors' morals. The assembled body then passed judgment on each case, after which it decided the course of action necessary and proper for the reforming of immorality.

The local Klan's course of action in the reforming of personal conduct usually resulted in the chapter's appointing a select committee which remonstrated with the delinquent on the evil of his ways. If this approach failed to bring about an improvement in conduct, the chapter then reported him and his sins to the police, offering to those officials its full moral support. Should the law authorities fail to act (in which case the local Klan attempted to retire them from office and fill their places with individuals deemed more worthy, preferably Klansmen), and should the wrongdoer still remain unregenerate, the chapter then turned to a more extreme measure — ostracism, perhaps. The local Klan expected its program of ostracism to force the wrongdoer into self-imposed exile. An actual case of a chapter's use of ostracism is worth citing. In a town of an eastern state, a hard-working, rather reliable young man was engaging in an illicit sexual relationship with a notoriously wanton woman. Threatened by telephone that he would regret it if he did not leave his mistress within three days, he chose to remain with her. Four days later his employer fired him. The following day his landlord demanded an exorbitant raise in rent. The milkman no longer went to the door. The butcher failed to stop his wagon. Merchants treated him with rudeness in their shops, some telling him bluntly that his patronage was no longer desired. By the end of the week only one grocer (in defiance of a telephone warning) would sell the man food, and this storekeeper was shortly brought into line by the loss of nearly three-quarters of his trade. Within two weeks the local Klan's program of ostracism had fully proved itself. The newly-created pariah moved to a hovel outside of town, where a few friends gave him aid and comfort until he was able to find employment and settle down elsewhere.

Rarely did any local Klan resort to a physical disciplining of an individual who had offended against its moral ideas. When a chapter did so, the press naturally gave the incident a great deal of coverage. Following are some illustrations of the Klan's use of corporal punishment. In October, 1920, an attorney from Yonkers, New York, Peter McMahon, while in the South to assist a client in a dispute over an estate, was taken from a train at Trenton, South Carolina, and beaten by a gang of individuals dressed as Klansmen. On April 1, 1921, a Negro bellhop from a Dallas hotel was abducted by a group of hooded men who branded him with acid on the forehead with the letters "K. K. K." Two months later, in Tenaha, Texas, a woman believed to have been committing adultery was seized, stripped of her clothing, and tarred and feathered. Another resident of the state, a woman from Goose Creek, was kidnapped by hooded and robed men who cut off her hair and tacked the tresses to a post in the center of town. On July 16, 1921, a sixty-eight year old farmer was whipped in Warrensburg, Missouri. The following day, in Miami, Florida, an archdeacon of the Episcopal Church was whipped, tarred and feathered. A few days later a man and woman at Birmingham, Alabama, received a flogging at the hands of a mob. In August, 1921, in Mason City, Iowa, persons who "preferred to be known as the Ku Klux Klan" forced a Socialist, Mrs. Ida Couch Hazlett, from a speaker's platform into a car, drove her to the outskirts of the city, and threw her out with a threat of greater physical violence if she returned. That same month, in Tulsa, Oklahoma, a ne'er-do-well by the name of Nathan Hantaman was dragged by Klansmen from his residence to a waiting car which deposited him just outside the city, where he was whipped until his back was a swollen mass of ugly welts. On August 24, 1922, near Mer Rouge, Louisiana, while returning from a picnic, two arch-critics of the local Klan of that town, Filmore Watt Daniels and Thomas F. Richards, were seized by hooded men. Two months later the badly decomposed corpses of Daniels and Richards were found floating on nearby Lake La Fourche.[14]

Two points must be made regarding the preceding illustrations of Klan violence, as indeed of any case of Klan lawlessness. First, since the individuals committing the assaults were hidden behind regalia, they could just as easily have not been members of the secret order. Second, if the men who engaged in these outrages were Knights, they could have been taking action without first obtaining the approval of the local chapter as a whole.

Of all the methods used by the Klan in the 1920's to put into effect its program, the one concerning which the scantiest records of the secret order were left, the one about which contemporary observers had the most to say supported by the least evidence, and the one which later students of the organization tended to avoid treating, was its engaging in political activity. Thus it follows that of all the many important aspects of the Klan the least understood is its role in American politics. What various Knights have said about whether the order actually was, or should have been, in politics, will certainly shed light on that area of the Invisible Empire's activity.

CHAPTER III

THE KLAN ENTERS THE POLITICAL ARENA

The political influence of the Klan during the 1920's was far greater than its numerical strength would indicate. The order had developed into the most energetic leader of the many millions of Americans who adhered to a brand of politics derived from chauvinism and religio-racial antipathies.

In 1925 *The National Kourier,* an official newspaper of the Klan, declared that it would not be very long before all political parties would have to "reckon" with the Invisible Empire. There is in the remark an underlying note of rejoicing. Such exultation, however, pales next to any one of many boasts made by Klansmen regarding their organization's political power. Bragging there was about the tremendous influence the Invisible Empire would soon have on every branch of the local, state, and federal governments. This boasting of Knights about the political strength of their organization must have led the merely curious outsiders as well as the deeply concerned observers to ask themselves why Klansmen considered it so very necessary for the Invisible Empire to be a powerful political force in the nation, and how they believed their order could achieve such force.

As to why, Klansmen had a variety of things to say. First, the political power of the Roman Catholic Church had to be destroyed. The May, 1923, issue of the widely circulated Klan magazine, *The Imperial Night-Hawk,* petulantly told its readers, "Wails of indignation arise from Catholics about the Knights of the Ku Klux Klan taking part in politics, yet it is all right for Catholic fraternal orders to line up votes for Catholic candidates and support at the polls the policies of Rome." Later that year Evans felt compelled to announce that "until such time as the Roman Catholic hierarchy announces Christ's doctrine of supremacy of State over Church in governmental affairs, we shall steadfastly oppose the political interference of Roman Catholic organizations in political matters in America."

Second, whatever political influence the Negroes, Jews, and foreign-born possessed had to be checked. The deliverer (his name was withheld from publication) of one of the "Inspirational Addresses" of the Second Imperial Klonvokation, held in Kansas City, Missouri, in

September, 1924, noted: "They talk about eliminating the Klan from politics. When you have eliminated the Polish bloc from politics in America, and the Italian bloc, and the Negro bloc, and the Jewish bloc, . . . then with reason you can begin to talk about the elimination of other blocs. Speaking before a group of white supremacists in Atlanta on political conditions in that city, "Colonel" Simmons, in less than temperate phrases, put forward the Klan's method for stifling the politically stirring Negroes of the capital of Georgia in particular and of the nation in general:

"I am informed that every 'buck nigger' . . . who attains the age of twenty-one years, has gotten the money to pay his poll tax and register, and that . . . these apes are going to line up at the polls, mixed up there with white men and white women.

"Lord, forgive me, but that is the most sickening and disgusting sight you ever saw. You've got to change that. . . . [Klansmen] will go, if they can, to the Governor's chair, or the Presidency of this nation. There is only one way to stop it. That is to out-vote them. This is a sacred duty that we must measure up to. . . . Keep the negro . . . where he belongs. They have got no part in our political or social life."

Third, politicians who prostituted themselves, in any manner, in order to attain or maintain office must be denied positions of public trust. One leading Klansman, a well-known New York City physician, and an officer of the Fifth Avenue church to which he belonged, while having no right to speak officially for his fraternity, must have conveyed the feelings of every one of his fellow Knights when he said, "Everybody knows that politicians nowadays cater to all kinds of 'elements,' mostly selfish, some corrupt, and some definitely anti-American. They cater to the . . . bootleg vote, the vice vote, and sometimes even the violently criminal vote. What the Klan intends to do is to make them pay some attention to . . . the decent, God-fearing, law-abiding vote."] "Ability and purity in public life are our greatest objectives," a prominent Klansman declared about himself and his confreres during an interview conducted by a close observer of the order, Edward Price Bell of the *Chicago Daily News*. "Only ability and purity in public life, in our opinion," the Knight went on to say, "can save democracy. When we fight for these things, therefore, we are fighting for democracy."

How did Klansmen believe that their organization could become the powerful force in American politics they so desired? First, they satisfied themselves that just informing the public of the patriotic, religious, and moral aspects of the Klan's ideology could have a positive effect upon the nation's political morality. In his volume on the Invisible Empire, Leroy Amos Curry, an unsuccessful candidate for Congress from Oklahoma and one of the functionaries of the Disciples of Christ, wrote the following about the fraternal order of which he was one of the apologists extraordinary: "I believe that this great organization can render an immeasurable service to the people of this country when those seeking political office are led to a more elevated plane of thought and activity by the ideals of this institution. . . ."

Second, Knights attached great weight to the secret fraternity's effectiveness in directing the voting of the American electorate, both the Klan and non-Klan elements, through an organized information service. E. H. Lougher, a Klansman from Kentucky, while writing about the political hold of the secret fraternity on the Blue Grass State, contended that the Klan never attempted to "control" votes; it had a "higher, safer" program. "The Klan will educate and influence the public to vote for the best candidates in every election, regardless of party," he explained. "It has been demonstrated absolutely this can be done. Give people full and complete information on every candidate, who and what he is. Tell men facts about all issues from sources they can trust. Then leave it to them to form their own opinions and exercise their own judgment." In the October 27, 1923, issue of perhaps the most significant Klan magazine, *The Dawn,* there appeared an article by the Grand Dragon of the Realm of Illinois, entitled "The Attitude of the Ku Klux Klan Toward Politics and Political Parties," a portion of which follows:

"Let each Organization, Great Titan and Field Man immediately send in to this office their recommendations along political lines, National, State and County officers, for the approaching election for our careful consideration and investigation of the respective candidates as to their qualifications, experience, etc., with a view to disseminating that information to the Klansmen with our recommendation, indorsement or comment for their guidance at the polls, so that they may cast an intelligent ballot, predicated upon prior information, data, and investigation, showing the true facts about the respective candidates' qualifications or lack of ability to fill the position to which he aspires. . . . There is no excuse for the Klansman elector going to the polls uninformed as to who is running and who is best qualified for the particular position. This information can always be secured from these headquarters, as we make it our business to know who is running for office in this State. We are always ready, able and willing to give authentic information concerning all candidates for any particular office and with such information the elector can weigh their qualifications for himself and act accordingly, or even accept the recommendations of this office with full assurance that they are made impartially without preference to party alliances, but solely on the merits of the particular candidate endorsed [sic] and a vote for such a candidate would be intelligently cast."

Now and then a publication of the order went a step further than merely furnishing information of a political nature to help Knights decide for themselves what candidates to support. In one issue of *The Watcher on the Tower,* a Klan magazine published weekly in Seattle, Washington, there appeared a directive to the subscribers which read as follows: "Get behind the 100% candidates for your next commissioners. YOU KNOW WHO THEY ARE. One of the present incumbents must be defeated; one should have your support. For the Commissioner of Finance, if you do not already know who is worthy, ASK A KLANSMAN."

Third, Klansmen put their full trust in their order's unflagging determination and ever-increasing ability to swing elections by supporting or opposing — as a body — particular candidates or party tickets.[1] "Moving in solid phalanx at the ballot box," Klansmen resolved "to put men who are 100 per cent American in charge of the affairs of the nation," a pamphlet of the order by C. Lewis Fowler announced. During the period when the anti-Klan forces were working the hardest to prove the lawlessness of the Invisible Empire, one Knight, George Estes, wrote that "Neither the Klan as a body nor any of its individual members has perpetrated any crimes whatever except it be the crime of voting judiciously at the state elections." To the Klansmen of Kansas, Charles H. McBrayer, the Grand Dragon of the Realm of Kansas, issued this statement regarding elections in their state:

"Of course you realize that it is necessary for us to move in solid formation if we [are to] bring about the results we all desire. Therefore, it is considered best for all of us to refrain from pledging our support as an individual to any candidate, until after all information has been assembled, and the Klansmen in the state have expressed a sentiment for certain candidates. After this has happened, it will then be very essential that we all support the same candidate, in so far as political party alignment will permit."

Included in the works on the Invisible Empire by "Klanswoman" Alma Birdwell White of New Jersey, who enjoyed local fame as a lecturer, preacher, and founder of Bible institutes, were many political cartoons. One depicted a Klansman in full regalia, holding in his hand a club labeled "ballot," chasing off three characters whom he considered politically powerful — the anti-Prohibitionist, the Jew (attached to whom were tags reading "corrupting movies" and "immodest fashions"), and the Catholic priest; another portrayed a Knight, properly attired in the order's garb, wielding a huge club labeled "the ballot" against a hairy, boney-fingered, long-nailed hand marked "Rome," grasping for land entitled "U.S.A."; still another cartoon showed an army of Klansmen standing in quasi-battle formation as some of its number were battering down the walls of political Roman Catholicism with tremendous logs on which were written "mens votes," "womens votes," and "the ballot."

The Dawn also had its share of political cartoons. One very striking drawing, for example, entitled "If They are Wise a Word is Sufficient," was of the Republican elephant and the Democratic donkey, each of which had a worried look on its face, being told by the Klan (typified by a hooded and robed Knight), "Gentlemen, if you expect my support you must *First clean House.* Get rid of your rotten Politicians, and construct your platforms on sound American principles."

Last of all, Klansmen took it for granted that they should be ever willing, when duty called, to throw their "hoods into the ring." "When necessity demands that they [Klansmen] enter the political arena no motive other than that of service to others can actuate them," *The Dawn* declared. "A desire to bring about law enforcement; to wipe out immorality, to improve the public land system, aid in solving the immigration problem, — these are the things that will compel Klansmen to accept public office at the hands of that vast majority of their fellow Americans who have similar ideals of what public service means."

Interesting it is that practically every spokesman for the Klan who admitted that the organization was in politics denied it at some other time. While the material available in which Klansmen deny that their fraternity was actively engaged in American politics is not nearly so extensive as that in which they admit to it, it is, nevertheless, large enough to be taken into consideration and dealt with at some length. It must be noted at the outset, however, that even the little material available in which Klansmen disavow their order's being occupied with matters political fails to impress — because of what is said and how it is said — later students of the organization.

At the first annual meeting of the Grand Dragons, held in Asheville, North Carolina, in July, 1923, a Great Titan of the Realm of Texas delivered a paper emphasizing that the Invisible Empire was not in politics. He maintained that although the Klan demanded of its members a patriotism toward the United States which could not be proved other than by participating in the nation's politics, "the organization which we here represent is not a political organization."

From Lougher, the Kentucky Klansman, came this notably ambiguous declaration: "The Klan is not a political party. We believe that to identify the Klan with or espouse the cause of any political party would be fatal to the organization and to the real worth of the crusade. The Klan, however, is mighty active politically, and every Klansman is a politician in the highest sense of the word."

What did those who were best able to speak for the order—Simmons, Clarke, and Evans — offer to bolster the assertion that the Invisible Empire did not seek to participate in politics? Even in its early days the secret fraternity had been charged, mostly by newspapermen, with taking part in local and state politics. Thus it was that during the Congressional investigation of Klan activities held in 1921, Imperial Wizard Simmons felt compelled to make a statement magnificently unequivocal: "The Ku-Klux Klan is not a political organization, nor does it seek political power, although this has been charged against us." Uttered Imperial Kleagle Clarke: the Klan "is not a political party, it will take no part in political controversies, and it has nothing to do with partizan [sic] issues. Klansmen will follow the dictates of their individual conscience in casting their votes. As an organization, we have no candidates — no favored party."

Addressing himself to the task of demonstrating that the Klan was not in politics, Imperial Wizard Evans had more to contribute than Simmons and Clarke. To the question put to him during an interview conducted by Bell, the Chicago newspaperman, "What do you mean when you say the Klan, as such, will take no part in politics?" Evans replied:

"I mean that the Klan is not a political party. Klansmen may belong and do belong to all parties and to no party. Every Klansman knows his principles and he votes for the candidate or the party in whose hands he regards his principles as safe or comparatively safe. To be sure, Klansmen, like other men, will use their influence to have parties and candidates further their objects; and, equally to be sure, if a candidate appears in the political arena blatantly proclaiming his hostility to our order and his purpose to destroy it if he can, Klansmen are likely to vote against him."

At the Klonvokation held in Kansas City, Missouri, in September, 1924, Evans, after outlining the future aims of the order, shouted,

"The Klan is not in politics, neither is it a political party." He continued, "We will permit no political party and no group of politicians to annex, own, disown, or disavow us. Where our conscience leads us, we will be found, regardless of who we find in the different political camps." A few years later the Imperial Wizard again denied a link between the Klan and political parties. "Neither the Republican party nor the Democratic party . . . has ever directly or indirectly furnished a single dollar to the Klan for any purpose whatever. The Klan seeks no political preferment and has no political affiliations." Such was a portion of the statement issued by Evans in reply to the charge that the secret fraternity was being financed by the Republican national committee in order to gain its support against the Democratic party in the presidential election of 1928.

Prompted by reports from critics of the Klan as to irregularities regarding the order's finances, Evans came forward in October, 1928, with a promulgation, in which he first disputed that the organization was insolvent, next declared that the Klan would be able to prove that it was not spending any money in politics, and then added (as if an afterthought) that members of the Klan, including the Imperial Wizard, did not desire public office.

But of all the disavowals by Evans of the Invisible Empire's being in politics, the one that must have instantly arrested the attention of the contemporary observer of the order was made in Dallas, Texas, on March 12, 1926: "The policies of the Klan have been changed, and it is now completely out of politics. It is not interested in the candidacy of any man or woman." Perhaps Evans momentarily lost sight of the fact that being "now completely out of" an activity could mean only one thing—that it had once been engaged in the activity.

It should be emphasized that being a political party and being engaged in politics are not the same thing; the latter can stand independent of the former. The affirmation by Klansmen that their order was not a political party can be readily accepted. However, the assertion by Knights that although some of their confreres, like many other American citizens, actively engaged in politics, the Klan *as an organization* did not do so, is unacceptable. For there are facts to show that the Klan as an organization did make a serious effort to become a significant power in the nation's politics.

The secret fraternity came to realize that to achieve this goal of power it would be necessary to adopt the methods of an American political machine. From embracing such a policy the order suffered three deleterious effects — it aroused the wrath of the American public, which did not want a fraternal organization active in the political field; it had to rely upon whatever skill was possessed by its leaders, the overwhelming number of whom lacked political training and experience, and thus political acumen; it dissipated its energies on all sorts of matters political on each of the three governmental levels — local, state, and national.

CHAPTER IV

LOCAL CHAPTER ANTICS

The chances were that not long after a local Klan had been establish-ed it would find itself participating in the political affairs of the com-munity in which it was situated. The chapter would make special drives to procure as members municipal executives, city and county legislators, court officials, and police authorities. Then, too, if the chapter were strong enough to exercise the balance of power in elec-tions, it would place in public office candidates who were Knights or sympathetic toward the philosophy and methods of the order. Being successful in these endeavors meant that the chapter was able to obtain local legislation favoring its program and, perhaps more important, to secure its activities from interference from the law. Illustrative of the latter, sheriffs who were members of, or on friendly terms with, the secret fraternity could appoint deputies until every Knight in a partic-ular county was commissioned to preserve the peace; judges and pro-secuting attorneys who were Klansmen or pro-Klan could be of service if the chapter were brought to trial for acts of terrorism.

The participation of the Klan in state politics and in Congressional and presidential elections received an immense amount of coverage in the newspapers and magazines of the nation. Quite the contrary was true of the participation of the order in local politics. For one thing, such activity was less newsworthy. Also, it was more difficult to ascertain the facts of the case. The reason is twofold. First, leaders of the local Klans were tight-lipped about the activity of their organi-zation in the political affairs of the community. They were perhaps afraid of saying a bit too much, thereby antagonizing superiors ready with swift and heavy punishment, higher-ups who, by the way, every now and then permitted themselves to recite something quite revealing about the Klan's role in politics on the state and national levels. Sec-ond, although frequently easy to guess, it was impossible to prove which chapters had succeeded in placing Knights in public office, since the Klan, as a secret fraternity, never made known its member-ship lists.

The sole reason given by the Invisible Empire for its entering into local politics was a desire to "clean up" the municipality or county.

In June, 1923, the two leading magazines of the order, *The Dawn* and *The Imperial Night-Hawk,* ran the very same article emphasizing that one of the great principles for which the Klan stood and fought was "CLEAN municipal government!" Just a month later a Great Titan of the Realm of Texas happily announced that in municipalities which in the past had been "honey-combed with administrative graft . . . slowly but surely the campaign of the Klan for good government has made itself felt." The battle, however, was still to be waged. The following year a pamphlet of the order affirmed that in "local affairs" even more than ever the Klan demanded: "(1) law enforcement; (2) stopping private graft and the spoils system; (3) healthful environments in public schools; (4) clean moral surroundings for children."

A satisfactory method of studying the participation of the southern wing of the Klan in local politics is to discuss separately each state involved. Restricting the survey to the eleven states that comprised the Confederacy plus two of the border slave states where the southern political tradition has remained strong, Maryland and Kentucky, it appears logical to treat each in the general direction of from the Upper South to the Deep South, and from the Atlantic coast westward to the Mississippi River and beyond.

The most un-American state in Dixie, as measured by the Klan standard, was Maryland. There were some chapters of the secret order in the commonwealth, but they were so scattered and their strength so negligible that most Marylanders did not take them seriously. As a result, instances of newspaper coverage of the fraternity's participation in local politics were few and far between. Only one journalistic account need be brought forward for an indication of the way the local Klans of Maryland would attempt to interfere with the execution of the duties of a duly elected officeholder. On July 26, 1924, the chapter in Myersville, a village fifteen miles from Frederick, sent a threatening message to Judge A. T. Brust, stating that "something real" would happen if he showed publicly any sympathy toward the victim of a tar and feather episode, and if he did not release the persons held as members of the mob committing the outrage. Whether "something real" meant political retribution against Brust is open to question.

In the neighboring state of Virginia the order was more successful in winning the friendship and co-operation of the servants of local government. Chief Charles A. Sherry of the Richmond police department declared that he had never heard more patriotic speeches in his city than those delivered by Imperial Wizard Simmons. In 1924, in

Graham, in the southwestern part of Virginia, the entire police force actually marched in a Klan parade on Washington's birthday; the following year, in Danville, near the North Carolina border, mounted policemen led a public Klan procession. Such action on the part of the constabulary of the Old Dominion might be understood if one takes into consideration that a high crime rate among certain groups of the economically and socially depressed colored population made the police sympathetic toward the anti-Negro views of the Klan.

One Virginia policeman who was charged with and denied belonging to the Klan was Chief Charles Barney Borland of Norfolk. The affair soon became a *cause célèbre*. In the June 10, 1921, issue of the *Weekly News Letter*, an official confidential publication sent out by the Propagation Department headed by Imperial Kleagle Clarke, there appeared a communication from the Exalted Cyclops of the Norfolk Klan stating that Borland had been enlisted in the ranks of his chapter. Included in the Exalted Cyclops' extremely colorful picture of Borland's initiation into Knighthood was a description of the police official's thanking 300 fellow Klansmen after they rose to pledge their support in the enforcement of the law in the city. To all this the Chief of Police offered a vigorous denial, replying that his one and only experience with the Klan was giving permission to the order to hold a public mass meeting in the Armory Hall, which he did deign to attend.

In nearby Newport News a similar incident excited great public interest. This time, however, more than a half dozen city officials, both elected and appointed, were involved. In the *Weekly News Letter*, dated May 20, 1921, a Kleagle reported that in Newport News "we have the chief of police, the commonwealth attorney, the postmaster, the police court judge, members of the city council. . . ." Chief of Police Campbell and the other civil authorities designated by the Kleagle promptly denied that they were or ever had been members of the Klan.

What of the secret order in local elections in Virginia? In the August, 1921, open primary in Richmond the candidate of the Democratic party for Commissioner of Revenue was John E. Rose, Jr. The interesting aspect is that Rose, a member of the City Council, had openly boasted of membership in the Klan. Civil servants of Richmond who were Knights were credited with having swung the victory in the primary to Rose; these were one-third of the aldermen, several members of the Common Council, a score of firemen, and about twenty-five policemen.

In Staunton, the birthplace of Woodrow Wilson, the local Klan held on July 7, 1924, the type of parade for which the secret fraternity had become famous. The reason was to celebrate the outcome of a recent municipal election. Of the candidates sponsored by the chapter for public office in Staunton, fully 80 per cent had been elected. A statistic such as this raises the question of whether these candidates would have been elected without Klan support. One could answer that seekers of public office who were approved and aided by the Invisible Empire might very well have been popular enough to gather on their own the votes necessary to insure their success; and if the fraternity desired to make an election a referendum on the Klan issue, it would find that it could not obtain one, because in an election there is more than one issue, although this is admittedly not so usually the case on the local level as on the state or national.

R. Walton Moore, one of the most respected members of the House of Representatives since his entering that body in 1919, and H. Earlton Hanes, a lawyer who had served in the House of Delegates from Fairfax County for two terms, contended for the nomination for Congress from the Eighth District of Virginia in the Democratic primary of August, 1928.[1] Moore announced that he was backing for the presidency that year Alfred E. Smith, while Hanes remained mum on the subject. Since Smith was the enemy of every Knight, it is no wonder that Hanes promptly gained the support of the secret fraternity within the Eighth District, which in the words of one competent political reporter was "rather badly infested with Klansmen." Notwithstanding the support Hanes received from the Klan, Moore's distinguished political record got him the Democratic nomination, and he went on to victory that November over his Republican opponent.

Over the Appalachians in Kentucky the Klan was far less important in local politics than it was in Virginia. In the Blue Grass State the secret order was unable to gain the confidence of the judiciary. Circuit Judge Carl Henderson in his charge to the grand jury in opening the 1921 fall term of the Hopkins County Court at Madisonville asked for a complete probing of the activities of the Klan in the area; Judge A. T. W. Manning in Circuit Court in London, Laurel County, on June 1, 1924, delivered a scathing rebuke to the fraternity, and then promptly excused from jury duty two men who acknowledged membership in it; in his charge to the grand jury at the opening of Circuit Court in Somerset, Pulaski County, in the fall of 1924, Judge H. C. Kennedy condemned the Klan, saying that there was no room in the county for such an organization.

So too did various civil executives criticize the Invisible Empire. For example, following announcements in the August, 1921, issues of the local newspapers advertising for recruits for the Klan, Mayor George W. Smith of Louisville made a statement condemning the order and asserting that he would use "every lawful means to prevent and suppress its growth in our community." The Board of Public Safety, acting in accord with the mayor, refused the fraternity permission to hold a meeting in the city.[2]

However, this was not the last that Louisville heard of the Invisible Empire. In the municipal election of 1925 the Democratic party was forced to switch the head of its ticket as a result of the Republican Campaign Committee's offering the Democratic mayoralty candidate, William T. Baker, $1,000 if he could prove that he was not, nor ever had been a member of the Klan. Two days before opening of the polls, Baker admitted he had been a Knight at one time, and withdrew from the race. Joseph T. O'Neil, former Judge of the State Court of Appeals, was selected in his place. In the extremely close election contest O'Neil lost out to his Republican opponent, Arthur T. Will. The backers of Will viewed the victory as stemming from the rift in the Democratic ranks.

The Paducah municipal election of 1923 should be noted. Wynn Tully, the Democratic candidate for mayor, had taken a leading part in the move to prevent a Klan speaker's being given a permit to lecture in the city. After hailing Tully for his action, the *Paducah News Democrat* forecast his election, since the Klan in a scolding campaign against the Democratic mayoralty candidate had "thrown many Republican and Independent votes to him." Tully was the only man on his ticket who was not elected. A spokesman for the Invisible Empire declared that "the fact that all other candidates on Mr. Tully's ticket were elected, shows conclusively that his act in aiding the faction that attempted to stop the Klan speaker brought about his downfall."

In Tennessee the influence of the Klan on the local political scene was obvious and direct. Speaking for the Knoxville chapter of the order, in April, 1922, C. Lewis Fowler declared that it was in the city hall and on the police force. He said further that the local chapter, as a powerful political force, was going to make certain that the Negroes of Knoxville were never given the chance to hold public office.

Although the picture of the strength of the local Klan in Knoxville as given by Fowler cannot be taken as fully true because of the ax that the Knight obviously had to grind, descriptions of the weight of the order in two other cities of Tennessee, Johnson City and Chattanooga, can be more readily accepted, since they are related by men who had left the Invisible Empire after having been most active in it. Ex-Kleagle Henry Peck Fry told of "a man who stood very high" in the local Klan in Johnson City during the early 1920's who, after first having talked about holding a parade of hooded and robed Knights, and then having been reminded of the provisions of the Code of Tennessee against wearing of masks in public, replied that this made no difference since the Klan controlled the politics of Johnson City. "We will parade anyhow," he concluded. "Nobody will dare stop us." Stetson Kennedy, who wrote widely-acclaimed exposés of the Klan of the 1930's and 1940's, was once told by ex-Knight J. B. Stoner that "back in 1924 the Klan was extremely strong in Chattanooga and at that time elected city judge McGoy, sheriff John Tate, and others."[3]

The 1923 municipal election in Memphis makes a good case study for one interested in the participation of the southern wing of the Klan in local politics. The Memphis chapter of the order had been very active in the past,[4] and in the fall of that year was busily urging every Knight in the city to vote the ticket which it as a body had endorsed. For every office — from mayor to alderman — the local Klan had tapped a candidate. On November 1, just one week before the election was to take place, a crowd of Knights marched to the court house, entered the office of John Brown, the election commissioner, and insisted that additional officials be appointed to serve at the polls in order to "preserve some semblance of fairness" in the forthcoming political contest. On November 9, when all the returns were in, Mayor Rowlett Paine and his entire administration but one (a city judge), running on the anti-Klan platform, had been re-elected. The sole incumbent who lost the race did so to the Klan-supported Clifford Davis. Davis owed his victory very clearly to the fact that the anti-Klan vote was badly split for city judge, three factions dividing the opposition. The *New York Times* described this decisive defeat of the order in the Memphis election as "the biggest black eye the Klan has yet received in Southern territory east of the Mississippi." Further, the newspaper said that everywhere in Tennessee the Klan was losing its influence in local politics, and predicted that although the order would poll a considerable vote in the 1924 elections, it would not be a controlling factor.

The prediction of the *New York Times* came true. Perhaps the outstanding feature of the local elections of 1924 in Tennessee was the poor showing made by the Invisible Empire. For example, in Shelby

County, of which Memphis is the governmental seat, the candidates whom the Klan backed did not even carry the rural districts, which had almost been conceded to them, and they failed to make inroads on the control of the county court.

Eastward, in the Carolinas, the Klan was able to make little headway in local political affairs. However, in North Carolina there was a mayor or two who was something more than friendly to the order and its members. When in the fall of 1924 the chapter in Ahoskie, a very small town in the coastal region, planned to stage a public demonstration, Mayor L. C. Williams "promptly" gave his assent to a parade and other exercises chosen for the occasion.[5] In Goldsboro, Mayor Edgar H. Bain once spoke of the order in terms as glowing as those a Kleagle might have used in recruiting members. The Mayor's remarks were the result of a report that the local Klan in Goldsboro was considering giving two wealthy Negroes of the city who had left for New York in Pullman berths an unwelcome reception upon their return for having dared to ride in such a conveyance. Dubbing the story "just a rumor circulated and accepted by outside newspapers," Mayor Bain went on to say that the secret fraternity stood "for fairness to all and above all things upholding of the law."

Available records pertaining to the local Klan in Raleigh, the capital and one of the largest cities of the Tar Heel State, point to the chapter's having on its membership list civil authorities, and attempting to put into office men friendly to its philosophy. During the hearings of a dramatic legal case of September, 1924, having to do with embezzlement from one of the city's most prominent stores, City Detective Joe Wiggins was forced to admit that he was a member of the Invisible Empire. About this time the local Klan in Raleigh was conducting a campaign to "clean up" the city. One of Raleigh's leading anti-Klansmen, the distinguished ex-Secretary of the Navy Josephus Daniels, away on vacation, was kept informed of the chapter's activities by his son Jonathan. The young Daniels wrote his father that in order to gain its objectives, "the Klan demanded the resignation of [Chief of Police A. E.] Glenn and dictated the selection of J. Winder Bryan. They are now planning to demonstrate beyond a shadow of a doubt that the change is a fine one and that it has long been needed."[6] That Glenn *was* replaced by Bryan in 1924 can be proved; that the local Klan of Raleigh was responsible for the turnover cannot be.

In South Carolina the Klan was close to impotence. This is interesting, for of all the states of the Old South, South Carolina was the most southern politically, the state of nullification and secession. In a two day investigation of the commonwealth made in late 1923 by a *New York Times* correspondent, few of the score of well-informed South Carolinians with whom newspaperman talked placed the order's strength at more than 10,000. In two-thirds of the counties there seemed to be no Klansmen and in the other one-third the number was insignificant compared with the total population.

The only important instance in which the issue of the Klan in South Carolina local politics had been raised was in the 1923 Charleston municipal election. John P. Grace, running for re-election as mayor, charged toward the end of his campaign that the secret order was behind the effort to unseat him. This was accepted by competent political observers to be a last minute effort on the part of the incumbent to rally the Catholics and Jews of the city to his support. Grace was badly defeated and the voters who retired him to private life included some of the most distinguished citizens of Charleston of the Catholic and Jewish faiths. Here is one of the very best examples of a politician using the Klan issue as a "red herring." In this instance the anti-Klan charge fell short of substantiation and the candidate failed to gather enough votes.

Although the Klan reached the height of its power in the area to the west of the lower Mississippi River and in the Middle West, the order remained throughout the 1920's a political force in its home state, Georgia. The Empire State of the South was fairly dotted with chapters, all of which attempted to gain the friendship and co-operation of the municipal and county politicos, and many of which were successful in this endeavor. On June 18, 1921, there was a public meeting in Rockmart, a sleepy little city in northwestern Georgia, with the principal speaker of the evening being Colonel J. Q. Nolan of Atlanta, who talked on the aims and operation of the Klan. What is noteworthy about the meeting is that seated on the platform with Nolan were J. A. Fambro, the mayor of Rockmart, members of the City Council, and two Knights of the Realm of Georgia.

In the July, 1926, issue of *The Forum* there appeared a captivating account of the efforts of Julian Harris, son of the beloved author, Joel Chandler Harris, and owner and publisher of the *Columbus Enquirer-Sun*, to defy the local Klan in Columbus. *The Forum* article related that when Harris purchased the newspaper in 1921, there were in the city on the Chattahoochee about 500 Klansmen, and the order was actually endorsed by the mayor and the chief of police, and permitted the use of the armory above police headquarters for its meeting place.

If Georgia was the home state of the Knights of the Ku Klux Klan,

Atlanta was the home city. A widely-circulated southern Negro week-ly, the *Norfolk Journal and Guide,* reported in the fall of 1921 that it was rumored that all members of the city government were members of the Invisible Empire. To such a charge Imperial Wizard Simmons had this to say during the Congressional investigation of the Ku Klux Klan in 1921: In Atlanta "after searching investigation by the . . . papers, it was found that only three officials in the county belonged to the klan, and a small number of the council, although many of those interviewed said they would like to belong to the klan, as they knew many citizens of Atlanta of the highest type who were members."[7]

One official who belonged to the secret fraternity was John A. Boy-kin, Solicitor-General of the Atlanta Judicial Circuit. In a letter to Simmons written on October 10, 1919, congratulating him on the showing made by the Klan in a parade in Atlanta that day, Boykin concluded, "Though it is seldom my privilege to attend the Klan meet-ings, because of the most pressing and grueling duties, when crime is rampant and there is unrest throughout the world, I want you and my brother Klansmen to know that I am with you in spirit."[8] Although Boykin never admitted that he was a Knight, the internal evidence of this communication (in the complete letter the Solicitor-General refers to his "brother Klansmen" three times) leads one to the conclusive inference that he was a member. The *New York World* once, by the way, noted that in Atlanta Boykin's membership in the Invisible Empire was taken for granted, and certain facts surrounding his election to his office were taken as evidence of the political power of the Klan in the capital of Georgia.

In the Democratic primary in Atlanta in 1922 the Klan became a serious issue. Chief of Police Beavers, seeking the nomination for mayor, issued a challenge to all his opponents, but particularly to Councilman Walter Sims, alleged to be a candidate put forward by the local Klan,[9] to state their positions on the fraternal organization. Beavers promised that if he were elected mayor he would use every lawful means in his power "to fight any improper influence the Klan may seek to exert in politics, or any hand it may seek to take in the affairs of this city. . . . " Sims won the nomination as the Democratic candidate for the chief municipal post of Atlanta, defeating not only Beavers but James G. Woodward, three times mayor of the city. The opposition to Sims by leaders of the Catholic Church and of the reform elements of Atlanta who were against the councilman because of his public acts of religious intolerance failed to triumph over the backing of the Klan that he received.

In the 1924 campaign for the judgeship of the Superior Court of Fulton County, of which Atlanta is the county seat, candidate L. F. McClelland charged that his opponent, Judge Gus H. Howard, had made the Klan, of which Howard was an acknowledged member, an issue in the race. Declaring that he himself was not nor ever had been a Knight, McClelland felt sure that numbers of men, "100 per cent Americans," who had joined the Klan as a fraternity would now agree with him that the order's "recent active entry into the political arena removes it from the realms of fraternal organization to that of a political party." Howard won the election.

Considering the fact that during the 1920's the Klan in Alabama drew nationwide attention as a participant in state politics, it is interesting that there were remarkably few newspaper accounts of the activity of the order on the local level in the Gulf state. Efforts of a political nature were indeed expended on this level; the newspapermen were perhaps so engrossed in writing up an account of the Klan in state politics that they did not have sufficient time to delve into activity on the local scene, a story considered to be less newsworthy. Be that as it may, there is one newspaper article in particular, a treatment of the 1927 mayoralty election in Montgomery, that should be turned to. In this contest in the capital of Alabama, William A. Gunter, the incumbent, was elected to the post over J. Johnson Moore, a candidate nominated through Klan influence. During the last days of the race, James Esdale, Grand Dragon of the Realm of Alabama, traveled to Montgomery from Birmingham, where he practiced law, to aid the Klan-supported office seeker. At political meetings held throughout the city by both factions numerous charges and counter-charges were indulged in. At the conclusion of his campaign, Gunter asked the citizens of Montgomery point-blank whether it was their wish to be governed by "the invisible empire or by a government of, for and by the people." The vote was more than two to one in Gunter's favor.

In Florida practically all Klan activity in local politics was channeled into preventing the Negroes from exercising the franchise. In a host of towns and cities in that state chapters of the order regularly staged just before elections extensively advertised parades, the object of which was to intimidate the colored population into staying away from the polls. In Jacksonville, on the night of October 30, 1920, for example, one such public spectacle took place; about 500 hooded and robed Knights silently marched through the streets, despite urgent requests from national Negro organizations to the local police department and city officials that the parade be prohibited.

Pertinent to the story of the Klan in Florida attempting to prevent the Negroes from participating in elections is an incident that occurred in Ocoee, a hamlet in Orange County. Three weeks prior to the November, 1920, elections, the local Klan sent word to the Negroes of Orange County that they would not be allowed to vote, and that if any member of the colored community attempted to cast a ballot, trouble would certainly ensue. Mose Norman, of Ocoee, refusing to be deterred by such threats, went to the polls, where he was overpowered, severely beaten, and ordered to go home. This episode incited a white mob to storm through the colored section of Ocoee, where it participated in an orgy of incendiarism, resulting in the loss of twenty houses, two churches, a school building, a lodge-hall, and dozens of Negro lives.

Three years later, in Miami, a few days before the municipal election of April, 1923, a broadside was distributed in the Negro section of that city. It read as follows:

> "Beware!
> Negro Citizens, as long as you keep
> your place, we will protect you,
> > But
> Beware! The Ku-Klux-Klan
> > is Again Alive!
> and EVERY NEGRO who approaches
> a polling place next Tuesday
> will be
> > A MARKED MAN
> This is a white man's country, boys,
> so save your own life next Tuesday
> > Ku-Klux-Klan,
> > Miami Chapter
> P. S. Don't think for a minute that
> we don't know you. A white man
> will be at every polling place with
> his book. DON'T GET IN THAT BOOK."

What must not be overlooked is that this handbill could just as easily have been distributed by individuals not belonging to the Klan, who took advantage of the threat which the secret fraternity afforded to intimidate Negroes into staying away from the polls.

In Mississippi the Klan was negligible as a factor in local politics.

However, throughout the 1920's Knights in Mississippi were full of hope that someday individual chapters in the state would employ political activity to carry out the order's program as successfully as they made use of Klannishness, charitable enterprises, and terrorism. A typical expression of this aspiration of the local Klans of Mississippi was penned by the Exalted Cyclops of Vicksburg in the May 13, 1921, issue of the *Weekly News Letter*: "The reason why everybody here has taken so keenly to the Klan is due to the fact that years ago the Jews and Roman Catholics formed a liaison with the liquor interests and have had politics in this city throttled, and it is our intention to whip and rout them at the polls when the next election comes around in 1922. We intend to put these un-American elements out of office precisely as other communities have done."

Across the Mississippi River in Arkansas the record of the Invisible Empire's participation in local politics was a long and full one. Election clashes between Klan and anti-Klan factions were bitter, there being no better example than the Little Rock municipal election of November, 1924. During this political race a report was current throughout the city that the local Klan had sent out "instructions" to its members that they support County Judge Charles E. Moyer for mayor. R. A. Cook, Exalted Cyclops of the Klan in Little Rock, emphatically denied any such action on the part of his organization, although he refused to discuss whether the local Klan as a body had endorsed Judge Moyer. In less than two weeks Cook was to make a statement vastly more interesting than this one. He declared that Mayor Benjamin Dunton Brickhouse, seeking re-election, displayed "rank ingratitude" in the attacks he made upon his opponent Moyer, J. A. Comer, ex-Exalted Cyclops of the Klan in Little Rock and now Grand Dragon of the Realm of Arkansas, and the Invisible Empire as a whole. In the past, Cook explained, Brickhouse had "sought and accepted the friendship of the local Klan and Exalted Cyclops Comer," but in this, his race for a fourth term, "he failed to obtain the backing of the Klan so he is very angry about it."

Weeks before the Little Rock municipal election Cook, speaking for his chapter, charged that during the Democratic primary of August, 1924, fraud was practiced in counting the votes cast in various precincts of Pulaski County, the governmental unit in which Little Rock is located. At a meeting of the local Klan, held on August 21, these details were presented: Klansmen who were members of the canvassing committee named to check the ballots cast in the primary discovered errors in the counting of the votes that were apparently deliberately made. Inasmuch as many of the errors adversely affected Klansmen who were candidates, especially for membership on the Democratic County Central Committee, the fraud must have been aimed at the secret order.

On August 26, the Pulaski County Democratic convention answered the charge of fraud. The meeting, packed with anti-Klan delegates who listened attentively to many verbal lashings of the secret fraternity, was the first at which a direct attack was ever made by the Democratic party in the county against the Klan. Scathing denunciations of the order were made by the chairman of the convention, Fred A. Isgrig, and the secretary of the County Central Committee, Frank H. Dodge.[10] These were both received with applause. Isgrig traced the history of the Little Rock Klan in politics, describing the fight it had made to obtain control of the school board, the county offices, and the membership of the state legislature alloted to the district. Dodge declared that no fraud was practiced in the primary, that the mistakes made in counting were unintentional errors resulting from the use of the long ballot. He pointed out further that the election judges and clerks were chosen with the assistance of Klansmen, including C. P. Newton, the Democratic candidate for county judge.

Before adjourning, the convention adopted a resolution, the conclusion of which stated: "Be it...resolved that we call upon the citizens not only of this county but upon all the counties of the state of Arkansas, to join with us in casting the Ku Klux Klan out of the Democratic party and forcing it to come out in the open, under its own colors as a Ku Klux Klan party, instead of seeking to hide its identity within the folds of the Democratic party."

On September 6th the Pulaski County Democratic Central Committee met to select its officers for the coming two years. On the Central Committee were both Klan and anti-Klan factions striving to capture the chairmanship and secretaryship. With the anti-Klan membership at about 190 and the Klan membership at approximately 75, it is not surprising that the personnel and philosophy of the newly-elected Central Committee was quite hostile to the secret fraternity's participation in the local politics of Pulaski County.

About this time, in the eastern part of the state, another battle was being waged by Klan and anti-Klan forces within the Democratic party. When the St. Francis County Democratic Central Committee convened on August 15 to canvass the returns of the recently held primary, notice of protest was filed by three of the defeated candidates. The petitioners were all backed by the local Klan and each alleged irregularities in counting; they were J. G. Sanders, W. J. Lanier, and C. R. Hine, candidates for sheriff, county judge, and county treasurer, respectively. The contested cases came to an end on October 11, when Circuit Judge John W. Wade decided against the petitioners after a trial lasting nine days and including the examination of several hundred witnesses. Each of the three Klan-supported candidates, as a matter of fact, finished the hearings with a much smaller vote than he had when he had started.

During the trial of the three petitioners some highly interesting details of Klan politicking in St. Francis County were brought to light. It was proved, for example, that the local chapter of the order had held its own elimination contests for Klan-endorsed nominees for the various offices in the Democratic primary, with all the contestants having been required to sign a pledge to support in the primary those of their number who won the elimination contests. It was shown, too, that the local Klan had undertaken the payment of poll taxes of individuals known to be in favor of the same candidates it backed.

The Klan, however, scored at least one political victory in Arkansas in 1924. In the Democratic primary of August for nomination for Congress from the Third District, J. N. Tillman decisively defeated E. G. Mitchell, who ran on an anti-Klan platform. Of the nine counties in the Third District, the only one Mitchell carried was Searcy, where for some time there had been a strong anti-Klan movement.

In Louisiana the Invisible Empire seems to have expended so much energy in endeavoring to regulate the morals of the inhabitants of the commonwealth that it had too little left to attempt to dominate municipal and county governments. Nevertheless, two examples of Klan activity in local politics in widely separated parts of the state should be noted, for they are as interesting as they are instructive. The local chapter in New Orleans, a predominantly Catholic city exceedingly hostile to the Klan, found it expedient in September, 1921, to close temporarily its office after Mayor Andrew J. McShane and Commissioner Stanley Raye condemned the order as un-American. In December of the following year, in Haynesville, an oil town far to the north, the mayor and each member of the police force received a letter bearing the stamp of Klan No. 63 of Louisiana ordering them to resign. The charge: shielding bootleggers and lawbreakers.

Like so much else having to do with Texas, there is only one word to describe the political power of the Klan on the local level during the 1920's—that word is "big". To begin with, in Beaumont, in the southeast, not far from the Louisiana border, the local Klan announced in the spring of 1922 that it would thereafter function as a political machine. The chapter published a statement proclaiming its intention to place in office Knights or sympathizers with the order. Quite soon after this was done a Citizens' League was formed to thwart the chapter's declared ambitions. From that point on there occurred rivalry between Klan and anti-Klan forces such as a city had seldom seen.

Judge W. H. Davidson of the Fifty-eighth District Court swore that he was escorted to the Klan meeting place in Beaumont by Deputy Sheriff George Wallace, where Sheriff Thomas Heslip Garner was waiting to tell him that "everybody wanted him in" and that "at the next meeting night he would be made a member." The judge, by the way, was quick to add that he refused to consider membership in the organization. Another jurist had a much less pleasant experience with the local Klan; that is, if it was the order that was at fault. Anti-Klan City Judge J. A. Pelt was tarred and feathered in April, 1922, by a hooded band of men. The Citizens' League charged the secret fraternity with committing the act. The city commissioners offered $1,000 for the arrest and conviction of any member of the mob responsible for the outrage, and Mayor B. A. Steinhagen made known his desire to "get those cowards who hid behind masks, whether or not they belong to the Ku Klux Klan."

Steinhagen said a good many other things to provoke the Knights of Beaumont. For example, he issued a statement declaring that while the City Commission did not presume to dictate to those in its employ regarding their affiliations with any organization, he himself felt that the membership of a municipal employee in the Klan was inimical to the public good. In 1924 the order was able to congratulate itself on vanquishing this great political enemy, Steinhagen. In the municipal election of April 1, the mayor was defeated for re-election by J. A. Barnes, a young attorney. Barnes, while not belonging to the local Klan, had its full endorsement in the campaign.

If the political power of the Klan on the local level in the Lone Star State was big, so too was the consequent fight put up by the opponents of the Invisible Empire. Reference to four separate communities should suffice to illustrate the point. When, in September, 1921, Mayor Stanton Allen heard that the local Klan intended to parade in his town of Bartlett, which lies about ten miles north of Austin, he hurriedly issued a proclamation forbidding it and ordered the city marshall to arrest any hooded and robed individuals who appeared on the streets. The chapter made no effort to carry out its announced purpose of marching. On March 16, 1922, District Judge John F. Mullaly in his charge to the grand jury at Laredo ordered a complete investigation of the Klan in that city. He instructed the members of the jury to summon every city, county, and federal officer in the area and question him as to membership in the fraternity, which he criticized as "an unlawful organization gotten up for purpose of violating the laws of the state." On the very same day, in Austin, Judge James R. Hamilton in Criminal Court found Police Commissioner J. D. Copeland in contempt of court for refusing to answer questions relating to the Klan and to his alleged membership in it—questions put to him previously by the Travis County grand jury. The court imposed a fine of $50, and ordered Copeland to jail, where he was to remain until he answered the questions. Asserting its belief that the Klan should disband in the "public interest," the Travis County grand jury on April 14, 1922, filed with Judge Robinson in Criminal District Court at Houston a report declaring that it had initiated a thorough investigation of the order.

Regarding the establishment of the Klan in Dallas in the early 1920's, John William Rogers, in his history of the city, writes that "It was plain that in local politics . . . the hooded organization was making itself felt." Such a remark becomes an understatement when compared with any number of others on the political power of the Klan in the city of Dallas and surrounding Dallas County during this period: "There the word of the Klan officials is law." "They [Klan leaders] take in all the policemen, every city or county official . . ." "It is claimed that every officer of the city and county of Dallas is a Klansman . . ." "For the next two years [1922-1924] we lived in a community where every city and county office was held by a member of the Klan or by a man who had made peace with it."

Probably the most serious threat to the political activity of the Klan in the Dallas area was the Dallas County Citizens' League, formed on April 15, 1922. This organization adopted resolutions deploring the existence of a secret order that engaged in terrorism. It also demanded that both holders and seekers of public office denounce the Klan. To all candidates for office in Dallas County and to some candidates for the federal Congress an extensive questionnaire was sent by the Citizens' League, the first three queries of which were: "(1) Are you now a member of the organization known as the Ku Klux Klan?; (2) Is it your purpose or intention to affiliate hereafter in any way with the Ku Klux Klan?; (3) Are you in sympathy with the purposes, practices, and objectives of the Ku Klux Klan?"

Naturally, some of the most interesting aspects of the political activity of the Klan in the city of Dallas could be witnessed only at election time. For a more balanced view of the part played by the Klan during elections held in Dallas, as indeed in the entire state, it would be well first to take note of a remark in 1924 by the Grand Dragon of the Realm of Texas, Z. E. ("Zeke") Marvin: "During the term for which I accepted the responsibility of the chief officer of the Klan in Texas it has been my earnest desire to keep the Klan out of politics, but in each campaign a candidate has thrown battle against the Klan forcing the Klan to defend its principles there in support of a candidate who had not attacked the principles of the Klan . . . " Following are two examples of local Klan politicking in the city of Dallas during the 1922 Dallas County election. At the height of the campaign Judge Barry Miller, an outspoken critic of the secret order, was visited in his law office by three Knights (none was a resident of Dallas so as not to be recognized by the jurist), the spokesman of whom said, "Judge Miller, your record in Texas is well known and admired. You have many friends in the Klan who would not want to see you hurt. But we are here to warn you that you've got to stop attacking the Klan. You mustn't make another speech against it." At the tail end of the campaign, on August 25, the local Klan sponsored an election eve rally at the city hall auditorium. The meeting place was soon filled, and the overflow, consisting of 2,000 people, went into the street where it gathered around a truck drawn up in front of the broad steps of the building to form a speaker's stand. More than a half dozen Klansmen or Klan sympathizers in the two meetings orated in behalf of a host of candidates for county office, practically all of whom, including Shelby Cox, who ran for district attorney, were to be victorious at the polls.

On April 6, 1922, Mayor S. R. Aldredge of Dallas issued a statement in which he asked all city employees who were members of the secret order to resign from it immediately, and requested the local chapter to disband. An organization which brought discord to a peaceful city, as the Klan had done, should not be permitted to exist, the mayor argued. The following year, in the municipal election of April 3, the local Klan took full revenge on Aldredge for his hostility. The mayor with the rest of his ticket was defeated for re-election by an almost three-to-one vote. Aldredge's opponent, who spoke neither for nor against the fraternity, had received the heartiest endorsement of the local chapter.

Beginning with the election of 1924, it should be noted, the anti-Klan forces in the city of Dallas and in Dallas County began capturing several offices, and the political strength of the order in that area was on the way to being broken.

For a time the local Klan in Houston exerted almost as much influence in municipal affairs as did the one in Dallas. In the summer of 1921 a newly recruited Kleagle was told by his immediate superior, the King Kleagle, that the Houston chapter of the order had engaged in some terroristic activity, but felt quite secure from interference by the law because it "ran things its own way, as it had the mayor, the police force and practically all of the politicians." Houston's Democratic primary for 1923 supports the Kleagle's assertion. In the contest for the mayoralty nomination were Judge Murray B. Jones and Oscar F. Holcombe, who was seeking re-election. The former admittedly had support from the local Klan; the latter was understood to be a member of the order. In this campaign Klansmen must certainly have breathed easily, for the success of either candidate would prove politically advantageous to their chapter. Also, it should not be forgotten that during this period victory in a Democratic primary in Houston, as in the rest of the "Solid South," was tantamount to victory in the general election to follow. It was Holcombe who won the nomination.

The experiences of three men who sought to hold the office of sheriff in different parts of Texas during the 1920's interestingly illustrate the efforts made by the secret order to place and keep in constabular posts Klansmen and Klan sympathizers. When the sheriff of Collin County, in the northeastern part of the state, was asked in the early 1920's to join the local Klan, he replied that he had better not do so lest his oath as a Knight conflict with his oath of office. He was then informed that if that was all that bothered him, he need not be further concerned, since if the chapter decided upon any illegal action his fellow Klansmen would make every effort to safeguard his conscience by executing it without his knowledge. Soon after his election in 1920 as Sheriff of Young County, not far from Collin County, John Sayce posted a notice inviting the Klan to co-operate with him in enforcing the law, but stressing that he would always be cognizant of his position as the duly constituted supreme police authority. Mob violence, whether committed by Klansmen or anyone else, it was added, would not be tolerated. The local chapter of the order reacted negatively to this; it was instrumental two years later in Sayce's defeat for re-election by a four-to-one vote. In the 1922 Democratic primary in Travis County, of which Austin is the governmental seat, Charles Hamly made a bid for the nomination for sheriff on a vigorous anti-Klan platform.

It was his contention that a sheriff, by the very nature of his position, must oppose the secret order, since it sought to take the law into its own hands. Hamly's chief opponent for the nomination rejected completely the viewpoint that a police official must be opposed to the Klan. This individual was none other than the incumbent, W. D. Miller, who months before had admitted to a grand jury that he was a member of the Invisible Empire.

Not long after the Klan had taken root in the Lone Star State, the Representative from the Fifteenth Congressional District in Texas denounced it as an organization that was totally foreign to the American way of life. The Invisible Empire consequently made known its intention to defeat for re-election in 1922 this antagonistic legislator. Members of the local chapter of the order in their regalia gathered around his home and burned a cross; they sent him threatening letters. When the political campaign was over, the Representative found that he had been defeated in counties he had never before lost, including his own. Nevertheless, he was re-elected to the lower House. That individual was John Nance Garner, later to be Speaker of the House of Representatives and Vice-President of the United States.

A few generalizations on the relationship between politicians and the southern wing of the Klan can be set forth with good advantage. Politicians in a section of the nation where public opinion was not solidly anti-Klan faced the dilemma of deciding what stand to take on the secret order. Their position has been likened to that of one accosted on a dark street by a masked individual who said he had a gun and would shoot straight for the heart if his orders were not complied with. Few would attempt to find out whether there really was a gun, and fewer still, whether it was loaded.

In its reliance upon the threat of reprisal against recalcitrant politicians, a threat too perilous to be ignored but too vague to be appraised or offset, lay the secret of the political power of the Klan. The fear engendered by the order's threat naturally varied from one part of the nation to another. In many localities—New England, New York, the north central states, the mountain states, for example—politicians naturally felt immune to the vengeance of the Invisible Empire. In other sections of the country, however, politicians found that they could ill afford to "withstand an incalculable impact, of indefinite forces, from an invisible source, and at an unexpected time." Such a section was, of course, the South.

Throughout the South chapters of the secret fraternity affixed a stamp of approval to candidates for office, often when it was unsolicited and sometimes when it was actually refused, usually by those who believed that they had over the years made their political position secure enough. The Klan delighted in picking a winner. However, if a chapter chanced to support a defeated candidate, it made sure to broadcast an alibi, for whatever the outcome of an election, the Klan considered it imperative that others be convinced that its influence had been preponderant.

The individual who in his successful quest for political office had sought and received the support of the Invisible Empire frequently found himself regretting the liaison. After the Klan helped elect the candidate to a position of public trust, it could remind him of his indebtedness *ad infinitum, ad nauseam*. Worse than that, it might inform the politico that if he did not comply with its wishes, whether political or otherwise, it would tell the public (in such a manner as to leave the impression that the information came from another source) of their relationship. Realizing the imminence of political death if he did not "play ball" with the secret order, the officeholder more often than not succumbed.

After having had a decade in which to gain an historical perspective of the southern wing of the Klan in politics, E. E. Callaway, in the February, 1938, issue of *The American Mercury,* saw a salutary aspect of the politicians' consorting with the secret fraternity, even if it meant their becoming members. The contributor to this influential magazine held that there was no question but that thousands of the ablest politicians of the South, sympathetic with neither the philosophy nor the methods of the Invisible Empire, associated themselves with local Klans for purely political reasons. That was possibly the best thing that could have happened at the time, according to Callaway, for if these men, in the final analysis neither weaklings nor demagogues, had not come to terms with the secret order, they would have been defeated, and the very worst element would have been elected. Thus the result would have been the thorough domination of southern politics by others, men who would have encouraged both racial and religious intolerance, rather than restraining them. Callaway's proposition does, at the least, contain an element of truth—and the thought *is* comforting.

CHAPTER V

STATEWIDE ACTIVITIES

An alert traveller making an extended tour of the South in the mid-1920's would probably have perceived as he made his way from the Upper South to the Deep South that the Klan was an increasingly important factor in the field of state politics. If this observant traveller had in fact become aware of that, then surely he would have noticed something more striking—the existence of three "pockets" of especial Klan strength in Georgia, Alabama, and Texas. Each of these "pockets" is discussed in this chapter.

In the early 1920's Klan officials were wont to brag about the link between the Invisible Empire and the legislative branch of the federal government. In a letter to an anti-Klan Southerner, dated January 1, 1920, Imperial Wizard Simmons declared that "among the Klan's most appreciated and loyal members now are members of Congress." Mrs. Tyler, while on a shopping spree in New York City in the fall of 1921, took time off to tell a newspaper reporter that although she was not at liberty to disclose any names, it was quite true that many officials of the United States government were Knights. Two years later in the Klan magazine, *The Dawn,* there appeared the following:

"Many Congressmen who went to their home unfavorable to the Ku Klux Klan will return to Congress as members of the great American organization . . .

"Engrossed as they were with legislation and other official duties some of the leaders are said to have accepted unfavorable newspaper stories as true accounts of the Klan's activities and the background of its principles.

"The return home has enabled them to learn first hand of the real regard in which the Klan is held by true Americans. Members of the organization have presented its claims of merit successfully so that there is no question but what the already large Klan representation will be materially increased."

More extreme than all this was the assertion, frequently made by Imperial Kleagle Clarke, that the Klan would one day soon be in actual control of the United States Congress.[1]

With the boasts of these Klan leaders in mind, the student of the secret order would do well to pause over the actions of two Georgians who served in the Congress during the early 1920's. When "Colonel" Simmons made his first appearance before the House Rules Committee conducting an investigation of the Klan in 1921, William D. Upshaw, Democratic Representative of the Fifth District of Georgia,[2] in spite of the remarks of the chairman of the committee that Simmons needed no introduction, delivered a bombastic address of presentation, full of phrases such as "his sterling character," "his every utterance as the truth of an honest, patriotic man," "a sturdy and inspiring personality," "incapable of an unworthy unpatriotic motive, word or deed," and "my long-time, personal friend."[3]

Upshaw's friendship for, and championing of, the Invisible Empire was of long standing. He declared that he always felt "a sort of wounded pride" in hearing criticisms hurled at the organization. On the stationery of the House of Representatives he once penned an un- dated note to Mrs. Tyler stating, ". . . I hope you, the Wizard and the Near Wizard will like it [an article to be published in the Klan newspaper, *Searchlight,* it appears]. If I can serve you and the *Searchlight* further please do not hesitate to command me." In the official organs of the Klan no representative ever got more coverage than Upshaw. Every piece of legislation he introduced, speech he delivered, article he wrote, public appearance he made seems to have been reported in the newspapers and magazines of the secret order.

But was Upshaw a Knight? Many contemporary observers of the fraternity thought so. One journalist, for example, included the Geor- gian in a group of "Kluxers in good standing"; another referred to him as "a Klansman who had been elected by Klan votes." Charges of membership in the Invisible Empire were never substantiated. This much, however, can certainly be said of Upshaw: if he was never a Klansman in fact, he was always a Klansman in spirit.

On the third day of the Congressional investigation of the Klan, Senator Thomas E. Watson of Georgia suddenly strode into the hearings room. All eyes turned upon this Democratic legislator widely known for his onetime leadership in the Populist party and his recent participation in the anti-Catholic crusade. Watson edged his way through the crowd, went up to "Colonel" Simmons, who was preparing to testify, seized him by the hand, whispered into his ear, and then turned around and sat down. A moment later he jumped to his feet, demanding the right to question the witness in the interest of "fair play." As he put a question to the Imperial Wizard, the Senator announced his firm resolve to protect the Klan from "any unjust attacks from anybody."[4] This was not the first time that Watson battled for the Invisible Empire. A month before he had publicly defended the order and denounced those attacking it.

In view of conduct such as this, it is no wonder that the Georgia Senator was charged with being a Knight. What reply did Watson make to the allegation? When he questioned Simmons during the course of the hearings on Klan activities held before the House Committee on Rules, he stated unequivocally that he was not a member of the secret order. On another occasion, however, when asked by one of his colleagues in the Upper House about his affiliation with the Klan, he boasted that he was called "the King of the Ku Klux in Georgia."[5]

In 1920 Thomas W. Hardwick, a former United States Senator, was elected governor of Georgia. During his two-year term of office, he demanded that the order discard the use of the hood, open its membership lists to the public and cease its terroristic activity. Naturally, he incurred the full wrath of the Klan.

When Hardwick sought re-election in 1922, the secret order was able to avenge itself. During the course of the campaign for the Democratic nomination for the governorship, issues of the Klan newspaper, *Searchlight*, full of anti-Hardwick articles, were distributed throughout the length and breadth of Georgia. Twenty trained and skilled speakers, under the direction of Imperial Klokard William James Mahoney, delivered addresses all over the state denouncing Hardwick. Imperial Kludd Caleb Ridley gave lectures against him. In the Democratic primary in July, the solid vote of the Klan went against the incumbent and for Clifford Walker, former Attorney-General of the state. The latter received the nomination and went on to victory in the fall over his Republican opponent.

Two years later, in the 1924 campaign for the Democratic nomination for the United States senatorship one issue took precedence over all others—that of the Klan. As a candidate for the nomination, former Governor Hardwick alleged early in July that a delegation from the Klan of the Realm of Georgia had called on Chief Justice Richard B. Russell of the State Supreme Court regarding the senatorial race. According to Hardwick, the deputation of Knights informed the Chief Justice that their order was determined that United States Senator William J. Harris should be re-elected, that it was willing to spend $500,000 to realize that end, and that it would be intensely displeased if Russell, able politician and proven vote-getter that he was, entered the Democratic senatorial primary.

Hardwick was not through making charges. In August he began to deliver speeches accusing Harris of being a member of the Klan. The latter ignored the allegation. But not for long. In early September Hardwick, in the course of an address, read a letter from Mrs. Elizabeth Tyler to the Exalted Cyclops of the local Klan in Cedartown, Polk County, dated March 16, 1922. In this letter Mrs. Tyler used the phrase "Hon. W. J. Harris, A. K. I. A." As every Knight in Georgia knew, and as the rest of the inhabitants of the state were to find out from Hardwick, "A. K. I. A." stood for "a Klansman I am." Confronted with such documentary evidence, Harris found it necessary to reply. He issued a statement in which he first declared that he was not nor ever had been a member of the Invisible Empire, and then expressed disgust that Hardwick should "stoop so low" as to read in the closing hours of the campaign an "alleged letter upon which he deliberately places a false interpretation."

Harris, receiving the Klan vote, won the nomination by one of the greatest majorities ever given a candidate in Georgia. With all but a half dozen of the 159 counties of the state going for him, the Democratic primary was indeed a landslide for the Senator.

At the close of 1922, with the failure of Hardwick to be re-elected Governor, the Klan of the Realm of Georgia had taken a new lease on life. Hardwick's pronouncements against the order's use of the hood, its keeping membership lists secret, and its practice of terrorism were now only to be laughed at by self-satisfied Knights. Clifford Walker was Chief Executive—and Clifford Walker was a friend of the Invisible Empire. From the time Walker acceded to the governorship, the secret order was given free rein in the Empire State of the South.

One of the candidates in the 1924 race for the judgeship of the Superior Court of Fulton County was Klansman Gus H. Howard. Having been appointed by Governor Walker to fill out an unexpired term, Howard was seeking to maintain the post at the hands of the voters. During the course of the campaign Walker ordered to be distributed to the women voters of the county copies of a personal letter, appealing to them to cast their ballots for Judge Howard. To no small portion of the femininity of the state the Governor's action was abhorrent. Mrs. Rebecca Latimer Felton of Cartersville, the first of her sex ever to sit in the United States Senate, took it upon herself to lead a female attack on Walker. She charged that it was the Klan that induced the Governor to have copies of the letter sent out. "It is said he is a Klansman. I do not know," Mrs. Felton declared caustically about Walker, "but it

happens he hangs up his 'hood and nightie' in the capitol of Georgia."
In a matter of a few weeks the Governor's relationship with the Klan
would be—if that was possible—even bigger news.

At the Second Imperial Klonvokation of the Klan, held in Kansas City,
Missouri, in September, 1924, an individual identified only as "the
Governor of a great State" delivered a speech entitled "Americanism
Applied." In the address the speaker bewailed, among other things,
the admission into the United States of "the lower type of foreigners"
and the "taking charge" of the 1924 Democratic national convention
by a "gang of Roman Catholic priests."

Upon seeing dispatches from the Klan convention referring to the
appearance of a governor during its proceedings, newspapermen were,
of course, instantly aware of a great story, which they diligently tracked
down to the executive mansion in Atlanta. It was found out that
after having announced that he was going to Philadelphia and Washington for a rest and vacation, Walker had traveled instead to Kansas City, accompanied by State Commissioner of Agriculture J. J.
Brown and State Commissioner of Fish and Game Peter S. Twitty, both
of whom were alleged to be Knights in good standing. Finally, on
October 13, 1924, Walker informed the press that "the Governor of
a great State" who addressed the Second Imperial Klonvokation was
he! That was not all. Walker admitted that he had joined the Klan
years before. He carefully explained, however, that he had never
taken any part in its council, and did not even know whether his membership was still in force.

After the Georgia Democratic presidential primary of March, 1924,
in which former Secretary of the Treasury William G. McAdoo beat
Senator Oscar W. Underwood of Alabama, much controversy arose
in the State Democratic Committee over the method of selecting delegates to the state convention to be held in Atlanta on April 25. In dis-
regard of the custom of the Democratic party in that state, McAdoo's
Georgia managers demanded the right to appoint all delegates to
the convention, maintaining that McAdoo's victory in the primary entitled him to have only delegates that were supporters of him. Certain
state committeemen insisted on holding conventions in their respective
districts so that delegates could be elected by popular vote, a procedure which was in keeping with the tradition of the Democratic party in
Georgia.

The latter point of view was distasteful to the Klan in Georgia, which
had given its full support to McAdoo in the primary. In order to help
McAdoo should the advocates of local autonomy in the choosing of

delegates be victorious, a proclamation was issued by Nathan Bedford Forrest, Grand Dragon of the Realm of Georgia, to all the Exalted Cyclopses under his jurisdiction. The document read as follows:

"You are hereby instructed to con the list of delegates named to the State Democratic Convention from your county and ascertain the names of Klansmen appearing thereon, and issue to them the following instructions: No district caucus will be held prior to the Convention. Such caucus will take place at the Convention as provided in the program. It is the earnest desire of Mr. McAdoo that his friends elect Major John S. Cohen as National Committeeman. Major Cohen is a high class Christian gentleman, a member of the North Avenue Presbyterian Church of Atlanta, and in every sense is acceptable to us, and we are assured that if he goes to New York the Klan's interests will be ably protected. Therefore before selecting a man for district delegate the Klansman voting should assure himself as to the stand such delegate will take with reference to Major Cohen and consequently the interest of the Klan. You will impress upon the Klansmen delegates the absolute necessity for their attendance at the state convention. Those who for financial reasons will be unable to attend should have their expenses paid by the local Klan. This is a time when everyone must do his bit and the Klan expects that everyone will do his duty."[6]

The outcome of the controversy over the method of selecting delegates to the State Democratic convention was that they were appointed by McAdoo's Georgia managers. At this convention, which had the task of choosing delegates to the forthcoming national convention of the Democratic party in New York City, the strength of the Klan was in evidence. Cohen was elected National Committeeman, and large numbers of individuals who were alleged to be Knights were included in the Georgia delegation to the national convention.[7]

Although it was the home state of the Klan, Georgia had never equaled certain other states in the number of Knights within its borders. With Evans' removal of Simmons, Clarke, and Tyler from the order in 1923, Georgia's supremacy in the Invisible Empire began to decline. Washington, D. C., came nearer to being the center of operations and authority of the order than Atlanta, the official seat. As a matter of fact, before the 1920's drew to a close the Klan actually transferred its national headquarters from the capital of Georgia to the capital of the United States.

In 1926, the Klan of the Realm of Georgia suffered a severe blow. In the Democratic primaries of that year every candidate who received the backing of the secret order went down to defeat—for the commissionership of Agriculture, judgeship of the State Supreme Court, United States senatorship, and governorship. In the first gubernatorial primary J. O. Wood, an avowed Knight, finished last in the voting, and in the "run-off" of October 6, the anti-Klan banker and physician, L. G. Hardman of Commerce, far outdistanced his sole opponent, pro-Klan John Holder, chairman of the State Highway Commission. "Imperial Wizard Hiram Evans trembles in his capital. Georgia, the seat and heart of his empire, has revolted," editorialized the *New York Times*. Nevertheless, the order still exerted political influence in the small cities of Georgia, was still sought after as an ally by various candidates for state office, and remained powerful enough to play an impressive part in the commonwealth during the national election of 1928, when the Democratic party's candidate for the presidency was a Catholic, Alfred E. Smith.

During the 1920's the Klan in Alabama received widespread attention for its participation in state politics. When Senator Oscar W. Underwood of Alabama made a bid for the Democratic presidential nomination in 1924, he did so on a stand in favor of the adoption by the national convention of an anti-Klan plank. As a matter of fact, the Senator went so far as to prepare such a plank (it was patterned after the anti-Know-Nothing plank adopted by the Democratic national convention of 1856) and have it read to the delegates assembled in Madison Square Garden in New York. While seeking the nomination the Alabaman had fiercely assailed the Klan and its policies—once in Houston, again in Boston, another time in Cleveland, and finally in New York.

For hurling such defiance against it, the Invisible Empire proclaimed that it would force Underwood out of politics. The Klan magazine, *The Dawn*, declared that Alabama Klansmen "are going to romp on Oscar Underwood so hard in the elections that he won't get to first base." On the same point, an official newspaper of the Klan, *The Fiery Cross*, reported, "They will take it out in hard swatting when the time comes. The Alabama Senator will think he has struck a Texas cyclone . . . " At the Klonvokation of the Klan held in Kansas City, Missouri, in September, 1924, the delegation from the Realm of Alabama, after scoring Senator Underwood for his anti-Klan utterances, vowed that it "would retire him in 1926." During an open air meeting called by the local Klan in Birmingham, on October 15, 1924, to initiate individuals into the order, 7,000 Knights cheered wildly while a coffin containing the body of Underwood in effigy was "laid to rest " through a trap door on the speaker's platform.

Underwood's term was to expire in 1927. He postponed announcing his intentions regarding the 1926 Alabama Democratic senatorial primary until he had made a thorough survey of the political scene. When he did speak it was to make known his retirement to private life. Filling the seat in the United States Senate vacated by Underwood was a young attorney from Birmingham, Hugo L. Black.

The Klan claimed the credit for Underwood's withdrawal from politics. In the January, 1928, issue of *The World's Work*, Evans went so far as to describe the Senator's removal from public life as one of the "outstanding achievements" of the order.[8]

Another series of events highlight the participation of the Klan in Alabama politics. One member of Governor Bibb Graves' administration of 1927-1931 was Charles C. McCall. A Knight, he was elected Attorney-General in the fall of 1926 with the full backing of his secret fraternity. Before taking office, McCall created a furor throughout the state by announcing that he had determined to appoint to the post of assistant attorney-general James Esdale, Grand Dragon of the Realm of Alabama.

The State Public Service Commission protested against the appointment, declaring in an open letter to McCall that the primary job of the assistant attorney-general was to supervise all cases coming before it, and since Esdale was without any experience in such matters, he would only hamper the work of the commission. McCall reminded the commission that responsibility for the efficient discharge of the duties of the position under question rested by law not upon the Public Service Commission, but upon the attorney-general.

It was Esdale himself who put an end to the affair. After a conversation with Andrew G. Patterson, the president of the Public Service Commission, in which he was told of the highly technical nature of the work pertaining to the commission, Esdale decided to write the Attorney-General-elect the next day declining the appointment. Esdale was reported as saying that after learning about the duties of the assistant attorney-generalship, he would not accept the post at any salary. Governor-elect Graves, who Edsale maintained had promised to endorse him for the office, remained silent.

In its very first year the Graves administration was discomfited by an outbreak of Klan lawlessness. First one county, then another, became the scene of tar and featherings, whippings, and brandings. In one county, Crenshaw, in the southern part of the state, "night-riding" was indulged in so frequently by hooded and robed mobs that a reign of terror could almost be said to have existed.

Distraught over this eruption of Klan violence, Attorney-General McCall quickly embarked upon a course of action which had all Alabama agog. He publicly confessed membership in the secret order, resigned from it,° assailed its brutalities, and then did everything in his power as the chief law officer of the state to halt its course of terrorism.

Graves was called upon to use the powers of his office to effect the liquidation of the secret order in Alabama; he refused even to consider such a course. Although the Governor did request the law enforcement staff of the state to aid local officials in the investigation of Klan violence and the prosecution of those found to be directly responsible for it, he placed in the Attorney-General's path many and varied obstacles. Into McCall's hands fell a document pointing to Graves' duplicity in the matter of stamping out Klan terrorism. It was a letter from James Esdale to Ira B. Thompson, Exalted Cyclops of the Klan in Luverne, dated September 14, 1927. The gist of the letter was that Esdale was certain that he would be able to convince Graves to render ineffective McCall's official course against the secret fraternity. (Why Graves hamstrung McCall was not made known to the public until a decade later, when the former admitted that he had joined the Klan before acceding to the governorship.)[10]

As a result of outraged public opinion and a more vigorous enforcement of the law against vigilance committees, Klan terroristic activity decreased rather quickly. But the Invisible Empire, Knights of the Ku Klux Klan, Realm of Alabama, was now irreparably discredited; its membership shrank steadily. The order remained vigorous enough, however, to play an important role in Alabama during the presidential election of 1928.

During the 1920's the Klan in Texas was as intensely active in politics on the state level as it was on the local. In 1922 the secret order made its influence felt quite dramatically in the race for the United States senatorship. In the Democratic primary of that year, which took place on July 22, many individuals aggressively sought the seat held by Charles A. Culberson, who after a quarter-century of continuous service in the Upper House campaigned for re-election in a less than forceful manner because of ill health. Three of the candidates for the nomination were admittedly pro-Klan, while the remaining four were anti-Klan. Included in the former group were an avowed Knight, Earle B. Mayfield of Austin, a member of the State Railroad Commission[11]; Robert L. Henry of Waco, a Representative who had recently terminated twenty years of service; and Sterling P. Strong of

Dallas, an attorney.   Those comprising the latter group were, in addition to Culberson himself,[12]   James E. Ferguson of Temple, a former Governor of the state; Clarence Ousley of Fort Worth, a former Assistant Secretary of Agriculture; and Cullen F. Thomas of Dallas, a prominent prohibitionist.

Before the primary took place the Klan of the Realm of Texas held its own elimination contest, voting upon the three pro-Klan candidates.[13] Having chosen a man, Knights all over the Lone Star State voted solidly for him in the primary.   This Klan-endorsed nominee received a plurality of the ballots cast.   The four anti-Klan candidates, having devised no plan of concerted action, remained in the race and split the majority vote among themselves.[14]   In accordance with Texas law, since no one candidate had received a majority, a second, or "run-off," primary was held on August 26, limited to the two individuals who had polled the greatest number of votes in the initial primary.   The contenders were Klan-endorsed Earle B. Mayfield and Klan-loathed James E. Ferguson.[15]   Mayfield won the nomination by 60,000 votes.

What happened to ex-Representative Henry in the race for the Democratic nomination for the senatorship should be noted.   Months before the primary was to take place Henry traveled to national Klan headquarters in Atlanta to see Imperial Wizard Simmons and returned to Texas with the Klan chief's personal endorsement for the legislative post.   Mayfield, in his attempt to get the support of the secret order, used a different tactic.   He first approached the Grand Dragon of the Realm of Texas and his cabinet, then the Great Titans of all five Provinces and their councils of advisors, and lastly the Exalted Cyclopses of many of the local Klans and their fellow officers.

Before Henry was aware of what was happening, the Klan in Texas had disregarded the wishes of the Imperial Wizard and settled on Mayfield as its choice for the United States senatorship.[16]   Henry, therefore, immediately terminated his affiliation with the Klan (it was alleged at the time that he had been a Knight in good standing but resigned in indignation from the order),[17] and went to the press with what he was wont to call a "double-cross."   The former Representative, embittered, remained in the race for the senatorship until the end.   It is not to be overlooked that he received the fewest number of votes in the initial primary.

A substantial group of Democrats, taking the position that Mayfield was the nominee of Klandom rather than of their party, turned to the Republicans with the suggestion of a fusion candidate.   E. P. Wilmot of Austin, a banker, already tapped by the Republican party

as its choice for the United States senatorship was withdrawn, and
Democrat E. B. Peddy, a Houston attorney, was substituted as the
Republican and Independent Democratic candidate. In the general
election on November 7 Mayfield won easily, receiving 264,260 votes
to Peddy's 130,744.

After the election Peddy charged that his opponent had won the
seat in Congress through gross irregularities. The case against Mayfield was brought before the Senate Committee on Privileges and
Elections, which conducted its hearings from May 8 to December 18,
1924. The most important charges submitted to the committee by
Peddy's attorneys were that voters had been intimidated by large
numbers of Mayfield campaigners; a vast sum of money, many times in
excess of the $10,000 which was the maximum permitted under Texas
law, had been spent by Mayfield forces in the two primaries; Mayfield
had not resigned from the Klan before his election, as he had always contended; and Klan funds had been put into a massive publicity
campaign in Mayfield's behalf.[18]

The testimony pertaining to the use of Klan funds to secure the
election of Mayfield formed a high light in the many sessions held by
the Senate Committee on Privileges and Elections. J. Q. Jett, who
had served the Klan variously as a recruiter in its Propagation Department, as a member of its secret service, and as a doorman at its national headquarters in Atlanta, declared that Evans (very soon to be
Imperial Wizard, he was at the time Imperial Kligrapp) had given a
memorandum for $25,000 to N. N. Furney, cashier of the order, who had
gone to the bank and returned with a handbag containing money.
Evans had wrapped the bills in paper and then departed with a visit-
ing group of Texans that was to be sent back home to work in Mayfield's behalf. Jett stated further that in a four-way conversation he
had engaged in, Evans had turned to Mrs. Tyler and told her that she
could well afford to present $100,000 from the Propagation Department
to the Mayfield campaign, in view of the fact that in 1922 Texas seemed
to be the only state in which a Knight could be elected to federal office.

The committee learned from Edward Young Clarke that when he
had been affiliated with the Klan as Imperial Kleagle, expenses of the
organization had had to be approved by a finance committee, with
which he himself had nothing to do, but from which he had heard
protests in the summer of 1922 regarding the amount of money Evans
had been spending in the Texas primaries then taking place.

At a dinner in Roanoke, Virginia, in 1922, Evans had remarked that
the Mayfield campaign had cost the Klan national headquarters be-

tween $80,000 and $100,000, according to F. M. Littlejohn, a former
Exalted Cyclops of the local Klan in Charlotte, North Carolina.

Furney testified before the committee in Mayfield's behalf that no
Klan funds had ever been drawn by Evans as described by Jett, and
that none had ever been dispatched to Texas for the Mayfield campaign.

J. E. McQuinn, assistant cashier of the Klan, had already taken the
stand before his immediate superior to deny that there was any item
in the books of the organization which pointed to contributions to the
Mayfield campaign in the primaries or general election.

The Senate Committee on Privileges and Elections heard testimony
on not only the efforts put forth by the national body of the secret
order to help elect Mayfield but also the efforts of the Klan of the Realm
of Texas and its individual local chapters. J. F. Collier, a public ac-
countant in Dallas, testified that in auditing the records of the local
Klan in that city in 1922 and 1923, he had found one item that was for
$11,102.04 under the entry "Educational and Propaganda," more than
half of which had been paid to Lowrey & Lowrey, a publicity outfit.
Collier explained that although he would be unable to declare under
oath for what purpose that amount had been paid to Lowrey &
Lowrey, he understood that that firm had handled funds for the local
Klan in Dallas in the political campaign of 1922.

H. M. Keeling told the committee that during a three-month period
in 1922 he had been, as an employee of Lowrey & Lowrey, in charge
of part of the publicity devoted to the political activities of the local
Klan in Dallas. "We were supposed," Keeling explained, "to create
sentiment in the county [Dallas] among voters in favor of the
entire klan ticket . . . It was really a Democratic ticket, but there were
certain gentlemen on that Democratic ticket who were different from
others. We called them the klan ticket." In reply to a question as
to where he had secured the funds with which to pay expenses, Keeling mentioned that he had received a number of checks from George
K. Butcher, an officer of the local Klan in Dallas, signed "George
King," and that they had been drawn on the account of a Benton
Joiner, as trustee. "George King" was a name belonging to no one in
the local Klan, Keeling went on, but on one occasion he had observed
Butcher from across the room signing a check, which when brought
over and handed to him had had the signature "George King".

Called as witnesses by counsel for Mayfield were two officials of
the Klan in Texas. F. G. Van Valkenburg, chairman of the finance
committee of the local Klan in Dallas, readily admitted that various
funds collected by the chapter to which he belonged had been used for

local political purposes during 1922, but stoutly denied that any part of it had gone to help elect Mayfield to the United States senatorship. As to the sum spent by his chapter in the 1922 political campaign, Van Valkenburg said it had amounted to approximately $700 a week. Admitting that Mayfield's name had been printed on the Klan ticket, Van Valkenburg hastened to add that Mayfield, upon finding out about it, had "raised Sam Hill." Brown Harwood, Grand Dragon of the Realm of Texas in 1922, affirmed that the only Klan funds he had ever spent in Mayfield's behalf was $6 or $8 for stationery and stamps.

After listening to this and other testimony of the most sensational kind, testimony that had attracted the attention of the entire nation, the Senate Committee on Privileges and Elections decided that there were no grounds for the unseating of Mayfield. As to the charges pertaining specifically to the Klan's role in bringing about the election of Mayfield, the committee was fully convinced of there being a lack of evidence conclusively proving illegal activity.

In 1924 the Klan again played an influential role in the state politics of Texas. In the Democratic gubernatorial primary, held on July 26, the secret order quite actively campaigned for Judge Felix D. Robertson of Dallas. One of the Judge's opponents was Miriam A. Ferguson.[19] Her supporters would have chosen her spouse if they could, but he was unable to have his name appear on the ballot. In 1917 James E. Ferguson had been impeached as governor and declared permanently ineligible to hold a state office. The chief charges brought against him were that he had misapplied $5,600 of public money, borrowed $156,500 from a "questionable" source, exerted improper influence on the Board of Regents, and violated the state constitution in his use of the veto.[20] It was thus that Mrs. Ferguson based her campaign (in the beginning, at least) on a fight for the vindication of her husband at the hands of the voters of the state.

With no candidate receiving a majority in the initial primary, Robertson and Mrs. Ferguson, as the individuals who had received the greatest and next to the greatest number of votes respectively,[21] were required to contend against each other in the "run-off." In the offing was one of the most heated political campaigns to take place in Texas. The group supporting Mrs. Ferguson adopted as its war whoop "Me for Ma"; that of Robertson, the core of which was composed of Knights, countered with "Not Ma for me. Too much Pa."[22]

Ferguson became campaign manager for his wife and made most of her political addresses for her.[23] Although he continually assaulted Robertson as the "Klandidate," Ferguson was personally not in too much disagreement with the anti-Negro, anti-Catholic, anti-Semitic, and anti-foreign-born philosophy of the secret fraternity. Consequently, in the campaign "Pa" Ferguson's fight with the Klan was directed against its desire for political domination in Texas (which clashed with his own), employing extra-legal methods to carry out its regulative program, and being an organization in which a hierarchy was able to accumulate much wealth and inordinate power. On their part, Robertson and those who stumped the state for him tactically ignored Mrs. Ferguson in their campaign speeches and denounced her husband as, for example, an "egregious scoundrel," an "insidious liar," and a "whiskey politician."

In the "run-off," held on August 23, Mrs. Ferguson obtained the backing of five of the seven candidates who were dropped after the initial primary, for each of the five was an individual of strong anti-Klan persuasion. Throughout the state large numbers of politicians flocked to Mrs. Ferguson's support in the second primary, not because they were for her but because they were against Robertson as the Klan-endorsed candidate. Despite the backing of the Invisible Empire, Robertson was defeated in the second primary by nearly 100,000 votes.[24]

At the State Democratic convention in Austin on September 2-3, the Klan was to suffer its worst political drubbing to date. The whole affair was completely controlled by the Ferguson wing of the party. So that the convention would be thoroughly anti-Klan in personnel, no delegation composed of a substantial group of Knights was seated and every attempt by certain delegations to have a friend of the order placed on the important credentials and platform committees was decisively defeated by the election of a substitute committeeman favorable to the Fergusons. The entire proceedings were filled with oratory mercilessly condemning the Invisible Empire and its methods. Evidently feeling that all this was not enough, the convention inserted in its platform an anti-Klan plank that was indeed not meant to be merely glanced at. It began: "The Democratic party emphatically condemns and denounces what is known as the Invisible Empire of the Ku Klux Klan as an un-democratic, un-Christian and un-American organization."

Mrs. Ferguson's Republican opponent in the general election, held on November 4, was George C. Butte, dean of the law school of the University of Texas. He was assailed by "Pa" Ferguson as "a little mutton-headed professor with a Dutch diploma," who was taking orders from Grand Dragon of the Realm of Texas Z. E. Marvin, "the same as Felix Robertson did." Butte, maintaining that the Fergusons were attempting to ride into the executive mansion in Austin on the Klan issue cried, "Mr. Ferguson calls everybody a Ku Klux who doesn't agree with him. He has even called me one."

The November 4 election, according to the *New York Times,* signalized "the greatest political revolution that ever took place in Texas." Tens of thousands of rock-ribbed Democrats cast a ballot for a Republican candidate for the very first time. Klansmen deserted wholesale the Democratic party to back the Republican gubernatorial nominee. That was not all. A number of anti-Klan Democrats, outraged at the thought that a governor removed from office on impeachment charges could return to power through subterfuge, had founded soon after the "run-off" an association called the "Good Government Democratic League of Texas," the purpose of which was to aid the Republicans in defeating Mrs. Ferguson in the general election. This newly formed organization of anti-Ferguson Democrats had given its full support to Butte.

Butte was defeated by more than 125,000 votes.[25] Mrs. Ferguson became the first female Governor of the state of Texas. An outstanding southern editor, George Fort Milton of the *Chattanooga News,* reflecting upon the election, penned, "The big trouble with the Klan politically is that its mere existence allows a vicious band of reactionaries to shelter behind the anti-Klan charge. . . . They offer a choice of two evils, and I will confess it is a terrible choice. Had it not been for the Klan Jim Ferguson never could have elected his wife (which means himself) in Texas."[26]

In addition to being marked by behind-the-scenes domination by her husband, favoritism in the granting of contracts for public works, and a policy of extreme liberality in dispensing of pardons, Mrs. Ferguson's two-year administration was characterized by a not unexpected hostility to the Invisible Empire. She practiced what she had preached as governor-nominate regarding the non-appointment to, and the removal from, state office of any individual who was a member of the Klan. Also, she convinced the legislature to pass a bill making it unlawful for any secret society to allow its members to be masked or disguised in public.

In 1926 Mrs. Ferguson sought re-election to the governorship. In the Democratic primary she was opposed by the youthful and able Attorney-General Daniel Moody. During the race Mrs. Ferguson and her husband, in an effort to make the Klan issue serve them as it had two years before, attempted to link Moody with the Invisible Empire. However, since Moody, first as District Attorney of Williamson and

Travis counties, and then as the chief law officer of the state, had diligently and successfully fought the secret order, the Fergusons could not effectively accuse him of being sympathetic to it. The nomination was given to Moody,[27] who went on to win by a 350,000 majority over his Republican opponent that fall.

During the primary campaign "Pa" Ferguson had declared that Moody's election would usher in "the rule of the Wizard." But a little over a week after he had won the Democratic nomination for the governorship, which was tantamount to victory in the general election to follow, Moody let it be known that he wanted the State Democratic convention to adopt a plank calling for the resignation of all holders of state office who were members of secret societies that tended to "breed hate, prejudice and religious jealousy."

As the second half of the 1920's got under way the disintegration of the Klan in Texas was quite evident. At the beginning of 1926, there were about 18,000 paying members of the order in the Lone Star State as compared with 97,000 a year and a half before, according to former Grand Dragon of the Realm of Texas Z. E. Marvin. That stronghold of the secret fraternity, Dallas, could account for a mere 1,200 Knights in 1926, whereas two years previously it was able to boast of 13,000. In none of the five provinces into which the Realm of Texas was divided did there remain the political power that elected Earle B. Mayfield to the U.S. Senate in 1922 and almost elected Felix D. Robertson to the governorship in 1924. "At the opening of this year [1926] not a province . . . could pay its help," Marvin was quoted as saying. Some observers even went so far as to declare that a Klan endorsement of an office seeker in Texas would mean certain defeat for him. While on a pleasure trip to New York City in the summer of 1927, Governor Moody, in reply to a question as to whether the order continued to be influential back home, declared unhesitatingly, "The Klan in Texas is as dead as the proverbial doornail." It was obvious that the fraternity's tremendous power in the state, both numerically and politically, was no more. Be that as it may, the Klan still possessed enough strength to affect the voting in Texas during the presidential election of 1928.

CHAPTER VI

DEBUT IN NATIONAL POLITICS

The national convention of the Republican party held in Cleveland, Ohio, from June 10 to 12, 1924, was a harmonious affair. The first and only ballot for the presidential nomination gave to the occupant of the White House, Calvin Coolidge, all but 44 of the 1,109 votes cast. When former Governor Frank O. Lowden of Illinois rejected the vice-presidential nomination awarded him on the second ballot, the convention promptly chose as Coolidge's running mate Charles G. Dawes, a Chicago banker who had served as the first Director of the Budget.

In the drafting and adoption of the platform, too, a minimum of discord was evidenced. Each plank accepted by the delegates was a true reflection of the views of their standard-bearer. Among other things, the platform praised governmental economy and tax reduction, declared against American entry into the League of Nations, endorsed the World Court, approved the limitation of armaments, pledged agricultural reform, recommended a continued restrictive immigration policy, and demanded punishment of all those guilty of the recently exposed corruption in government.

There were, however, circumstances concerning one area of the platform-making that did jar the serenity of the convention. R. B. Creager, a national committeeman from Texas and a member of the Committee on Platform and Resolutions, headed a small group which demanded of the party that it adopt a declaration against the Klan. The delegation from New York also favored an official denunciation of the secret fraternity. Dr. Charles F. Thwing, president emeritus of Western Reserve University, presented to the Committee on Platform and Resolutions a proposal signed by several prominent citizens asking for an anti-Klan plank. The seven-hour animated discussion by the platform committee regarding the inclusion of a plank condemning the order broke out at one point in a heated argument.

The most interesting aspect of the anti-Klan plank issue at the Republican national convention was an enterprise with which the delegates themselves had nothing to do. Sixty representatives of the Klan, headed by Evans and Walter F. Bossert, Grand Dragon of the

Realm of Indiana, traveled to Cleveland, where they set up head-quarters at the Hotel Statler. This deputation of the Invisible Empire threatened to "punish" Creager for his persistent attacks, and swore to remain on the scene until the platform committee completely rejected the idea of an arraignment of their order.

What the platform committee finally presented to the convention for its consideration was a plank, promptly adopted, which contained no direct and positive statements on the Klan, but read simply: "The Republican Party reaffirms its unyielding devotion to the Constitution and to the guarantees of civil, political, and religious liberty therein contained."

The Republicans heard from the sixty Knights who had gone to Cleveland more than their views on an anti-Klan plank. Nothing less than sensational was the statement which Klan headquarters at the Hotel Statler gave out on June 9. It read: "All of our boys throughout the nation will understand only one thing, and that is Senator James E. Watson [of Indiana] for Vice President — flat. We will deny any responsibility for the defeat of the Republican Party at the polls in November if Watson is not selected for Vice President, on the ground that he is the most available candidate to carry the Middle Western States which are necessary for the election of Coolidge."

Senator Watson immediately spurned the endorsement of the secret order, saying, "I don't belong to the Ku Klux Klan.[1] If they have issued a statement naming me, they have done it for the express purpose of injuring me. Such a statement was made without my knowledge or consent, and is wholly without authority from me or anyone having the right to represent me." Watson's advisors vigorously assailed the Klan pronouncement. Many of them, believing that the Senator's chances for the vice-presidential nomination (never very good to begin with) were now completely destroyed, urged him to release the Indiana delegation, which was pledged to him for that office. Watson refused to do so.

Thereupon Evans repudiated the Klan declaration as unauthorized and untrue: "The statement that the Knights of the Ku Klux Klan are demanding the nomination of any man to any office is unqualifiedly false. I am the only man authorized to authoritatively speak for the Klan, and I solemnly affirm that the Knights of the Ku Klux Klan is not in politics . . . and the statement appearing in the press attributed to me concerning Senator James E. Watson is without foundation of fact."[2] Here the matter rested.

Antipodal to the brief and tranquil Republican national convention was the Democratic one held at Madison Square Garden in New York; it lasted from June 24 to July 9 amid scenes of the grossest sort of antipathy and factiousness. Nothing could alter the fact that the Democratic party was violently split on a new political issue — the Klan.

Unlike the case with the Republicans, the Klan question could not be disposed of quickly and quietly. Historically and traditionally, there were two great wings of the Democratic party constantly at odds with each other — the South and the East. The former was rural, agricultural, overwhelmingly Protestant, native-born, prohibitionist, and conservative, while the latter was urban, industrial, heavily Catholic, of recent immigrant stock, anti-prohibitionist, and liberal. The issue of the secret order could do no other than to widen appreciably the gulf between the two wings of the party, for the South was the home of the Klan and the East the center of anti-Klanism.[3]

The proceedings of the first four days of the convention, however, gave no indication that actual calamity was to take place. Senator Pat Harrison of Mississippi, as temporary chairman and keynote speaker, and Senator Thomas J. Walsh of Montana, who had gained fame as chief investigator of the fraudulent leasing of naval oil reserves at Teapot Dome and Elk Hills, as permanent chairman, scored the Republican party. Both addresses were received with the enthusiastic applause of all delegates. The nominating speeches did contain allusions to the Klan issue, which triggered lively demonstrations from certain sets of delegates on the floor and visitors (the overwhelming majority of whom were anti-Klan New Yorkers) in the galleries.[4] But all this was quite natural.

It was not until the fifth day, when the Committee on Platform and Resolutions made its report to the delegates, that every Democrat knew for certain that his convention was hopelessly split into two camps. The chairman of the platform committee, Senator Homer S. Cummings of Connecticut, in a manner that betrayed fatigue and agitation, announced that the committee had reached unanimous agreement on all planks of the platform except two — one having to do with the League of Nations and the other with freedom of religion, speech, and press. The debate on the former, the convention was told, "though prolonged, was entirely amiable," while on the latter, it continued "all night long" becoming "more heated" as time went on, and finally "somewhat acrimonious."

After all the planks prepared by Cummings' committee had been read to the delegates, Permanent Chairman Walsh gave the floor to

Newton D. Baker of Ohio, Wilson's Secretary of War from 1916 to 1921, who proceeded to offer a plank drawn up by a minority of the platform committee which advocated American membership in the League of Nations. When the Ohioan had finished, William H. Pattangall, a leading politician of Maine, was permitted to offer an amendment to the "Freedom of Religion, Freedom of Speech, Freedom of Press" plank which had been endorsed by fourteen of the fifty-four members of the committee.

The minority proposed adding to the single-paragraphed plank reaffirming the Democratic party's "adherence and devotion" to "those cardinal principles" in the Constitution regarding freedom of religion, speech, and press the following two sentences: "We condemn political secret societies of all kinds as opposed to the exercise of free government and contrary to the spirit of the Declaration of Independence and of the Constitution of the United States. We pledge the Democratic Party to oppose any effort on the part of the Ku Klux Klan or any organization to interfere with the religious liberty or political freedom of any citizen, or to limit the civic rights of any citizen or body of citizens because of religion, birthplace or racial origin."

Then a duel took place in the convention hall. This combat between the supporters of each plank on the freedom of religion, speech, and press was fought with the deadly weapon of words under formal conditions of debate and in the presence of seconds on each side, the latter being hundreds of hissing, booing, laughing, screaming, cheering, hurrahing, applauding delegates and visitors. Nicks were suffered; blood was drawn. As first speaker for the minority plank, Pattangall believed that the principal difference within the platform committee arose from the question of whether the platform should be absolutely frank or not. If it was unwise to name the Klan it was unwise to put in the platform something that meant the secret order. At one point he uttered, "There is more in this matter than the mere naming of a secret organization. There has crept into American life so strong an influence in certain States that United States Senators told me last night that if the Klan was opposed by them they could not be re-elected to their seats in the Senate."

Bainbridge Colby of New York, Secretary of State under Wilson, was blunt as he could be for the minority report: "I am somewhat accustomed to the cowardice that invades the issue of the Ku Klux Klan, but I confess to my surprise that, seated on this platform, I am obliged to witness the hardihood (or shall I say effrontery?) of its open defense. . . . If you are opposed to the Ku Klux Klan, for God's sake, say so. . . .

I wish to record my dissent as a Democrat to the majority report. It does not satisfy my thought. It does not satisfy my manhood. It is no credit to the Democratic Party."

Governor Cameron Morrison of North Carolina, in support of the majority plank, began by defending the rights of the individuals who "mistakenly" belonged to the Klan. "Are we," he asked, "without trial and without evidence, in a political convention where only basic principles should be dealt with, to try, condemn and execute more than a million men who are the professed followers of the Lord Jesus Christ?" If the majority resolution were passed, the North Carolinian prophesied that "upon every stump upon which a loyal Democratic orator stands in the coming campaign he will attack the principles of the Ku Klux Klan, with reason, with logic, and it will wipe it from the face of the earth, in front of the onward march of the great Democratic party."

Former Mayor Andrew C. Erwin of Athens, Georgia, for the minority, spoke briefly. The convention could, he emphasized, by adopting the report of the majority, evade the issue, but such a course would, in effect, mean giving its approval to the activities of the Invisible Empire. Erwin pointed out: "You hear on every side, in the lobbies of the hotels, in the halls, and upon the floor of this Convention, that we should take no action relating to the Klan any more than we should take action relating to the Masons or Elks or any other secret organization. I cannot bring myself to this view of it; I have not heard of the Masons or Elks moving from State Convention to State Convention, from National Convention to National Convention, regardless of party, a highly paid staff of officials, lobbyists and spying investigators, with a view of controlling the acts of delegates chosen to represent the people of this Country."[5]

Toward the beginning of his twenty-five minute address in favor of the majority plank, William Jennings Bryan rapped, "Note, my friends, that they [endorsers of the minority plank] take our report, every word of it, and note also that we offered to take every word of their report but three. We said, 'Strike out three words [Ku Klux Klan] and there will be no objection.' But three words were more to them than the welfare of a party in a great campaign." He went on to say, "I am not willing to bring discord into my party. The Democratic Party is united on all the economic issues. We have never been so united since I have known politics. . . . Now, when we are all united and all stand with a dauntless courage and enthusiasm never excelled, these people tell us that we must turn aside from these things and divide our party with a religious issue and cease to be a great political party." For his peroration the "Peerless Leader" chose the following words: "It was Christ on the Cross who said, 'Father, forgive them, for they know not what they do.' And, my friends, we can exterminate Ku Kluxism better by recognizing their honesty and teaching them that they are wrong."[6]

So sounded some arguments from some speakers. Then the polling of delegates took place. For the nearly two hours during which it occurred the convention was in an uproar. Chairs were overturned. State standards were broken. Fist-fights were started. The roll call was interrupted time and again by delegates who wanted either to change their own votes or to challenge the accuracy of the final votes of their states as cast by their chairmen. From beginning to end the voting was close.[7] The final official tabulation showed that the entire number of votes cast was 1,083-6/20. The number of "ayes" was 541-3/20; the number of "noes," 542-3/20. Thus, the Democratic national convention rejected the inclusion of an anti-Klan plank in its platform for 1924 by the narrow margin of one vote.

Ultimately the platform as a whole was adopted by a *viva voce* vote of the convention. Among other things, the document lashed out at the corruption within the government during the Republican administration under Harding, defended the income tax against the Republican party's policy of increased tax reduction, advocated a lower tariff, endorsed the limitation of armaments, promised agricultural reform, proposed that a referendum be held to decide the issue of American membership in the League of Nations,[8] and reaffirmed the Democratic party's devotion to the principles of freedom of religion, speech, and press.

When it came to choosing a presidential nominee, the Democratic convention was once more ruptured by the Klan controversy. The candidate of the anti-Klan delegates was Governor Alfred E. Smith of New York. William McAdoo of California, who had achieved great prominence as Wilson's Secretary of the Treasury during World War I, was the choice of the pro-Klan delegates (and of the Klan itself), although he repeatedly denied any affiliation with the secret order and spoke out against much of what the organization believed in.

The balloting began on June 30. On the first ballot McAdoo obtained 431½ votes; Smith, 241; former Governor James M. Cox of Ohio, the party's standard-bearer in 1920, received 59 votes; Pat Harrison, 43½; and Oscar W. Underwood, 42½. The rest of the votes were divided among fourteen favorite sons. Soon the minor candidates dropped out, leaving the field to McAdoo and Smith. But as ballot after ballot was taken, and as day after day passed, neither the Californian nor the New Yorker was able to muster the two-thirds majority which the Democratic party had for almost a century ruled necessary for the presidential nomination. After the longest deadlock in the history of national political conventions, the delegates wearily chose on the 103rd ballot John W. Davis, a New York City corporation lawyer, who had during the course of his career served as Representative from his home state of West Virginia, Solicitor-General under Wilson, and Ambassador to Great Britain. For vice-president the liberal Governor Charles W. Bryan of Nebraska, brother of William Jennings, was nominated.

That the Democratic national convention of 1924 had been rent asunder heartened one group of politicians — the Republicans. One individual in the higher echelons of the G.O.P. was asked by a reporter what he thought the effects of the Madison Square Garden imbroglio would be. "Well," he smiled, "the Democrats might have done better by us, of course. They might have disbanded and gone home. But short of that they've done about all they could for Coolidge and Dawes."

Just as a deputation of the Invisible Empire had gone to Cleveland and set up headquarters near the scene of the Republican party's national convention, so did one travel to New York City to do the same for the Democratic party's. This time the Imperial Wizard was accompanied by a far greater number of individuals who ranked near the top of the Klan hierarchy. In a five-room suite on the fifteenth floor of the Hotel McAlpin, Evans conferred continually with a handful of Grand Dragons: Walter F. Bossert of the Realm of Indiana, James A. Comer of the Realm of Arkansas, James Esdale of the Realm of Alabama, Nathan Bedford Forrest of the Realm of Georgia, Fred L. Gifford of the Realm of Oregon, N. C. Jewett of the Realm of Oklahoma, and Z. E. Marvin of the Realm of Texas.[9]

Upon arriving in New York, the Klan officials made public their intention of having a voice in the choosing of the platform and candidates by the Madison Square Garden convention. These leaders let it be known that if they could prevent the Democrats, as they did the Republicans, from mentioning the Klan by name in the platform, they would credit themselves with an important victory. With the platform adopted, they would turn to preventing the nomination of anyone outspokenly critical of their order.

Although the Klan leaders refused to divulge the exact number of Knights sitting in the various state delegations, they did assert that in the impending fight to prevent the adoption of an anti-Klan plank, the Invisible Empire could count on the support of 85 per cent of the Georgia delegation, 80 per cent of the Arkansas, Kansas, and Texas delegations, 75 per cent of the Mississippi one, and more than 50 per cent of the Iowa, Kentucky, Michigan, Missouri, Ohio, Tennessee, and West Virginia delegations.

As to those delegates occupying seats in the convention who were at the time dues-paying members of the Invisible Empire, the *New York World* placed the figure at approximately 300. This newspaper also noted that "More than one United States Senator wearing a delegate's badge is suspected of K.K.K. membership." Every delegation, with perhaps three or four exceptions, had from two to thirty Klansmen or pro-Klansmen, reported the *Baltimore Sun* from one of its sources. According to the *New York Times,* Senator Earle B. Mayfield of Texas, a delegate-at-large from that state, and Virgil C. Pettie, a delegate-at-large from Arkansas, were said to be serving along with the more than a half dozen Grand Dragons on the inner council set up by Evans to decide Klan strategy at the convention. Representing his home state on the Democratic National Committee, Pettie was at the same time Imperial Klabee of the Realm of Arkansas. Although the Arkansan was the only member of the Democratic National Committee who admitted to belonging to the Invisible Empire, it was believed that at least two other national committeemen were Knights. The Klan was known to have "representatives" on the Committee on Platform and Resolutions. While it was the *New York Times* that took refuge in the word "representatives," the *Baltimore Sun* declared less cautiously that Texan Alva Bryan of the platform committee was a Klansman.

Soon after the convention began its proceedings, the Klan leaders decided that the progress of the fight against an anti-Klan plank warranted calling in reserves. Among the first to be contacted was W. A. Hanger, an attorney from Fort Worth. (It was said by those "in the know" that whenever in great trouble Evans summoned him.) Hanger was the chief counsel for Mayfield before the Senate committee which conducted the investigation of the charges of unlawful practices in the election of the Texan to the Upper House. When Hanger found it impossible to heed the call to New York because of illness in the family, Hollins N. Randolph, chairman of the Georgia delegation, and Alva Bryan acted in his place to help the Imperial Wizard.

With the defeat of the anti-Klan plank, Evans and his aides gave their full attention to the process of nominating the presidential candidate. Knights were notified by their leaders that if McAdoo were unable to win the nomination, the order would lend its support for that post to an individual not unfriendly to the Invisible Empire, Senator Samuel M. Ralston of Indiana. As a matter of fact, right from the beginning Ralston was more acceptable to some Klan officials, particularly Grand Dragons Bossert and Marvin, than was McAdoo. To their way of thinking, the former Secretary of the Treasury's chances of being nominated were slim indeed because of his having been retained by oilman Edward L. Doheny, who had benefited from the fraudulent leasing of governmental oil reserves during the Harding administration, and because of the bitter hostility to him of the pro-Smith East. Word of the Klan's eyeing Ralston for standard-bearer of the Democratic party got around, and the Senator felt it necessary to announce that he was not a member of the secret fraternity and that he challenged anyone to prove the contrary. Ralston's statement did him no political good; while it did not gain him the support of any important anti-Klan politicians, it lost him the favor of some influential Klansmen.

With the Republican and Democratic national conventions being a matter of history, candidates for office and party workers turned to electioneering. In a campaign speech made at Sea Girt, New Jersey, on August 22, Davis referred to the Klan in the following manner: "If any organization, no matter what it chooses to be called, whether Ku Klux Klan or by any other name, raises the standard of racial and religious prejudice or attempts to make racial origins or religious beliefs the test of fitness for public office, it does violence to the spirit of American institutions and must be condemned. . . . " After attacking the order, the Democratic candidate then expressed the hope that Coolidge would, "by some explicit declaration," do the same, and thus remove the Klan issue from the political debate.[10]

Although the Republican presidential nominee completely ignored the Klan question throughout the entire campaign, his running mate did pick up the gauntlet on behalf of the party. In Augusta, Maine, on the day following Davis' Sea Girt address, Dawes not only condemned any American organization that appealed to racial or religious prejudice, but went on to say that although "the Ku Klux Klan in many localities and among many people represents only an instinctive groping for leadership, moving in the interest of law enforcement, . . . it is not the right way to forward law enforcement."

Even before Davis and Dawes castigated the order, the standard-bearer of the new Progressive party,[11] the reform Senator Robert M. LaFollette of Wisconsin, in a letter made public on August 8, had stated: "I am unalterably opposed to the evident purpose of the secret organization known as the Ku Klux Klan, as disclosed by its public acts." Thus, before the political campaign of 1924 was half over, the entire nation had heard from Davis, Dawes, and LaFollette on the Klan.

In a statement issued on August 22, Imperial Wizard Evans declared that the strength of the Invisible Empire would be thrown against the candidacy of LaFollette. "LaFollette is the arch-enemy of the nation," the document read. "No man who endangered the success of his nation in time of war is fit to hold any office, much less occupy the position through which the country must stand or fall."[12] As to the nominees of the two major parties: "Coolidge and Davis are nationals and Americans, aides of the Klan in the attempt to 'Americanize America,' and for this reason the Klan will take no part in the political struggle as far as they are concerned." Since this statement was made public on the same day as, and obviously just before, Davis' Sea Girt speech, the Imperial Wizard was compelled to revise very quickly his opinion of the Democratic candidate.

The Klan was not the only organization to attack the Progressive party candidate during the election of 1924. Rather than forcefully coming to grips with each other on the basic questions of the day, the Republican and Democratic parties tended, increasingly so, to direct their efforts against LaFollette and his radicalism. As the campaign wore on the Klan issue was pretty much forgotten, although every now and then Davis in the midst of an address was interrupted by hecklers demanding that he review his position on the secret fraternity.

The election was a Republican landslide. Coolidge captured the electoral vote of every state in the East, Middle West (except Wisconsin), and far West; Davis carried only the "Solid South" and Oklahoma; LaFollette won the electoral vote of his home state alone. In popular votes, Coolidge received 15,725,016; Davis, 8,385,586; and LaFollette, 4,822,856.

Knights everywhere, with no small measure of pride, proclaimed their order responsible for the desolation of the Madison Square Garden convention and for the political defeat of Davis a few months later. Speaking for the Invisible Empire as no other individual could, Imperial Wizard Evans asseverated:

"Our enemies, and some of our friends, charge or credit us with the debacle of the . . . Democratic National Convention, and with the defeat of Mr. Davis that followed. There is some truth in the charge; to be sure, the Klan was not present as an organization or with an organized force of delegates on the floor of the convention, but it was present as an intangible force. Delegates were afraid of what we might do! Nor did we conduct any campaign against Mr. Davis, but his official repudiation of the mental attitude taken by the Democratic platform in regard to our organization, and his subsequent attacks on us, alienated hundreds of thousands of voters — and those not alone inside the ranks of the Klan."

Chapter VII

WAR AGAINST AL SMITH

On August 2, 1927, while vacationing in the Black Hills of South Dakota, President Calvin Coolidge called together a group of reporters to hand to each of them a slip of paper containing a dozen words: "I do not choose to run for President in nineteen twenty eight." This was indeed good news to all those members of the G.O.P. whose ambition it was to be the nation's Chief Executive. One of those aspirants — and by far the most "available" — was Herbert Clark Hoover of California. After having achieved great fame during World War I as Chairman of the Commission for Relief in Belgium and as United States Food Administrator, he was appointed Secretary of Commerce by Harding and was then serving in that capacity under Coolidge.

By the time the 1928 national convention of the Republican party began its proceedings in Kansas City, Missouri, which lasted from June 12 to 15, Hoover's nomination appeared inevitable. As had been expected, the Secretary of Commerce captured the prize on the very first ballot. Upon his receiving 837 of the 1,089 votes cast, a motion to make the nomination unanimous was easily carried. Selected to be Hoover's running mate was Charles Curtis of Kansas, majority leader in the Senate.

As had been the case in the 1924 convention, the drafting and adopting of the platform was accomplished with the barest amount of contention. Among other things, the platform praised governmental economy and tax reduction, recommended a high tariff policy, declared against American entry into the League of Nations, and demanded full enforcement of the Eighteenth Amendment.

The Democratic national convention was held in Houston, Texas, from June 26 to 29; it was a quite different affair from the long and acrimonious one of four years before. The dissension between the southern and eastern wings of the party still existed, but two events had taken place which made for peaceful convention proceedings. In a letter to George Fort Milton, editor of the *Chattanooga News*, made public on September 17, 1927, William G. McAdoo had declared that "in the interests of party unity" he would not seek the presidential nomination. Then, on September 23, leaders of the Democracy from eight mountain and Pacific coast states, the majority of whom were ardent McAdooites at the Madison Square Garden convention in 1924, had met in Ogden, Utah, where they endorsed the already booming candidacy of Alfred E. Smith. Thus it was that in 1928 the selection of the Governor of New York as the party's nominee met with merely token opposition.

Contending for the nomination in addition to Smith was just a handful of favorite sons, including Senators James A. Reed of Missouri and Walter F. George of Georgia, and Representative Cordell Hull of Tennessee. On the first ballot Smith received only 10 votes fewer than the two-thirds majority necessary for the nomination. Before another ballot could be taken Ohio switched its vote to the Governor, thus giving the party its standard-bearer for 1928. For vice-president the delegates chose Joseph T. Robinson of Arkansas, permanent chairman of the convention and minority leader in the Senate. As a Southerner, Protestant, and prohibitionist, Robinson balanced the ticket.

In contrast to what had taken place in the 1924 Democratic convention, the platform was drafted and adopted in an easy and quick manner. The document pledged the party to, among other things, a low tariff policy, agricultural reform, international co-operation (there was no mention of the issue of American membership in the League of Nations), and an "honest" attempt to enforce the Eighteenth Amendment.

In January, 1928, Imperial Wizard Evans prophesied that his order was going to be more strongly represented in the Democratic party's national convention of 1928 than it had been in the one of four years before. During forthcoming proceedings, Evans went on to elaborate, all the influence of the Invisible Empire would be directed toward an effort to prevent Smith's receiving the party's nomination.

Just before the opening session of the Democratic national convention a group of Klan officials, headed by Evans, arrived in Houston to set up headquarters at the Hotel Milby.[1] The Imperial Wizard authorized a statement to the press to the effect that his order was on the scene to fight for the inclusion in the platform of a plank pledging complete enforcement of the Eighteenth Amendment, and not to take part in the choosing of candidates.

With the adoption of the plank on the enforcement of the Eighteenth Amendment, Evans and his aides did participate in the contest over the selection of nominees. They attempted to halt the avalanche of votes for Smith, and failed. They then tried to prevent the choosing of Robinson for the vice-presidency, and again failed.[2] (It can be assumed that the Klan opposed the nomination of Robinson because a running mate who was a Southerner, Protestant, and prohibitionist would measurably increase Smith's chances of being elected.)

With the same audacity that he had used in taking credit for the Klan for the defeat of Davis in the election of 1924, Imperial Wizard Evans promised that the secret fraternity would bring failure to the standard-bearer of the Democratic party in 1928 should Smith be given the nomination. In order to make good the threat of the Imperial Wizard, the Klan as an active participant in the presidential campaign of 1928 employed a variety of methods and techniques. In the first week of July the local Klan in Wahouma, Alabama, a hamlet not far from Birmingham, held an anti-Smith demonstration to which the townspeople were invited. The high light of the evening was the hanging of the New Yorker in effigy. Before being strung up, the man of straw had a knife plunged into his throat, mercurochrome poured over him to heighten the effect of the "assassination," received a shot or two in the middle, and was dragged around the hall to receive vigorous kicks from vengeful Knights. After the "lynching," the more than 200 individuals in attendance listened to speeches by leaders of the local Klan denouncing the "steam roller" tactics at the Houston convention.

In a letter sent out to every local Klan under his jurisdiction, Amos C. Duncan, Grand Dragon of the Realm of North Carolina, requested that a fund of at least $8,000 be raised to fight Smith in the Tar Heel State. Before making the actual appeal for the money, Duncan carefully explained why it was needed: "I am immediately putting five more whirlwind campaign speakers on tour in this State, using them seven days per week until November 6th [election day]. I am having prepared literally tons of powerful campaign literature which you Klansmen must distribute during the final phases of this crusade to every voter in North Carolina. My office will function 24 hours per day until victory is won."[3]

Duncan's counterpart in Georgia also found it necessary to resort to an appeal for a campaign chest to defeat Smith in his race for the presidency. Grand Dragon Nathan Bedford Forrest contacted every Knight in the Empire State of the South, requesting from each a contribution of anything from $.50 to $5,000.

On a ten-acre plot in Virginia, stiuated but a few miles from the nation's capital, stood a huge electric sign announcing the support of the Klan of that state for the Republican candidate. Owned by the secret order, this tract of land was used throughout the campaign for Hoover rallies of Arlington and Fairfax counties.

Less than a week before election day the local Klan in Miami, Florida, condemned five of its members for lending support to Smith's campaign. The Exalted Cyclops of the chapter went so far as to call upon the most prominent Knight of the five, Louis C. Allen, a former sheriff of Dade County, to stand trial before the order for his "major offense."

The Klan during this presidential race undertook the distribution of a body of political writings; all of it, or practically so, was simply anti-Smith literature. Each of the writings can be put into one of four categories, according to the basis for its attack on the New Yorker: (1) his Catholicism; (2) his being a "wet"; (3) his Tammany connections; and (4) his so-called "alienism."

Of the total sum of anti-Smith campaign literature disseminated by the Klan, the largest — and most intemperate — portion had to do with the Governor's religious background. Smith as President would "no doubt fill every key position in the Republic with Roman Catholics . . . [and] no doubt leave the Army and Navy in the hands of Rome," the September 5, 1928, issue of the *Official Monthly Bulletin* of the Realm of Mississippi prophesied uneasily. In her book, *Klansmen: Guardians of Liberty,* which although written in 1926, enjoyed a wide circulation among Knights during the 1928 presidential race, "Klanswoman" Alma Birdwell White went a step further: if Smith ever occupied the White House he would so "manipulate the reins of government in behalf of the Roman Pontiff" that "Free speech, free press, free public schools . . . would soon be things of the past."

From the writings distributed by the order attacking the New Yorker on the other three counts, only a few excerpts need be brought forward to convey adequately the flavor of the assault. Regarding Smith's anti-prohibitionism, one issue of *The Kourier Magazine,* a monthly Klan periodical published in Atlanta, Georgia, contended that "the liquor interests and the private citizens who are 'wet in principle and in practice' . . . seek to overturn American law and to destroy the American Constitution. Gov. Smith has made himself their leader. . . ."

As to Smith's affiliation with Tammany, in another issue of *The Kourier Magazine* there appeared the following: "It is impossible to conceive that any of the great Democratic leaders of the past would consent to support such a man. Tilden, Cleveland, Bryan, Wilson — all these men denounced and fought Tammany Hall. There is no doubt that Jefferson and Jackson would have done the same if it had been what it is today. It is unthinkable that such men as these should accept the leadership of a man who boasts of his membership in an organization that has stood for graft, corruption, [and] alliance with crime. . . . "

Concerning Smith's "alienism," the pro-Klan newspaper, the *Washington, D.C. Fellowship Forum,* said to its readers: "Mr. Smith represents a body of voters who do not believe in . . . American principles and traditions; who wish another and a different set of ideas to become dominant in the nation. These un-American ideas go under the general title of alienism. Smith represents the attempt of alienism to win control of America."

A startling aspect of the battle for the White House in 1928 was the rabid attack upon Smith by a fellow Democrat — Senator J. Thomas Heflin of Alabama.' Addressing a gathering of nearly 10,000 Knights just outside Syracuse, New York, on June 16, 1928, Heflin vowed that he would do all in his power to prevent the Governor's receiving·the nomination of the Democratic party in its forthcoming national convention, for he did not want to see the presidency of the United States "becoming the tail to the Roman Catholic kite." Speaking at an open-air meeting of the Klan in the outskirts of Albany, New York, on the following day, the Senator asserted that it should be clear to everyone Smith must be denied the highest office in the land because he was a Catholic, a "soaking wet," and a Tammanyite.

Just three days before the Democratic convention began its proceedings, Heflin announced that he would remain silent throughout the campaign if the Governor of New York were nominated. But he failed to keep his promise. In the months that followed the Senator appeared before groups of Klansmen — in Ohio, in Illinois, in New Jersey, in New York, in Kentucky, in Pennsylvania — to embolden them in their opposition to Smith's candidacy.

During the course of the presidential race the question naturally arose of whether Heflin was a Knight. In September of the preceding year, in an address to the Lions Club of Mobile, C. M. Rogers, an Alabama state legislator, had assailed Heflin as a member in good standing of the Invisible Empire. That Rogers had been unable to substantiate his charge was of no import to the many millions of Americans who must have cared little about the distinction between Heflin's being actually a member of the Klan and his being merely an exponent of its tenets on the Senate floor and lecture platform. The issue of Heflin's alleged Knighthood was finally settled, but not until 1937, when Imperial Wizard Evans told the press that in the late 1920's the Senator had indeed joined the secret order.

Smith did not take these blows from the Klan without striking back. In an aggressive stumping of the nation, he scored the fraternity for the tactics it was using against him in the campaign. Addressing a group on September 20, in Oklahoma City, Oklahoma, where Klanism was still so deep-rooted and anti-Catholicism so widespread that his personal safety was a concern, the Democratic candidate mentioned that the following incident had recently come to light: The Grand Dragon of the Realm of Arkansas, in a letter to a citizen of that state, had urged Smith's defeat because of his religious faith, suggesting to the man that by voting against the Governor he would be upholding American ideals and institutions as established by the Founding Fathers. As to that kind of politicking, Smith concluded, "Nothing could be so out of line with the spirit of America. Nothing could be so foreign to the teachings of Jefferson. Nothing could be so contradictory to our whole history." A month later, on October 29, in Baltimore, Maryland, the New Yorker told with emotion the following to his audience:

"Recently I made a trip to the State of Indiana. I went there not only as the candidate of the oldest political party in the country but as the Governor of a sister Commonwealth. As we were passing along in the train I saw in the darkness by the side of the track a blazing cross, and one of the men in charge of the train told me that that was symbolic of the Klan's defiance of me.

"There is a fine state of affairs in this twentieth century, with all of our education and all of our culture. What excites in me the most of my rage is the hollow mockery of it — to raise between heaven and earth the emblem of Christianity as a defiance to a fellow-citizen, the Executive of a great State.

"So far as I am concerned, I would sooner go down to ignominious defeat than to be elected to any office in this country if to accomplish it I had to have the support of any group with such perverted ideas of Americanism."

Compared with the energetic campaign staged by Smith, the one conducted by the Republican candidate was rather easy-going. Not once did Hoover make express reference to the issue of the Klan's participation in the presidential race. He did feel compelled, however, to object to the attacks made upon Smith on religious grounds. In his speech accepting the nomination, delivered at Stanford University,

Hoover uttered, "By blood and conviction I stand for religious tolerance both in act and in spirit."

As had been so in 1924, the election was a Republican landslide. Hoover won the electoral vote of forty states, including his opponent's home state of New York, and five states — Virginia, Tennessee, North Carolina, Florida, and Texas — of the half-century old "Solid South." In popular votes, Hoover received 21,392,190 to Smith's 15,016,443.

It is not difficult to find the reasons for the outcome of the election. To the negative factors involved in the defeat of the Democratic nominee — the opposition to Smith because of his religion, his anti-prohibitionism, his Tammany connections, and his "alienism" — must be added the positive one of the belief on the part of many Americans that the general prosperity of the times was dependent upon continued Republican rule.[5]

It is difficult to assess the effect that the activity of the Klan had upon the outcome of the election, for there were other influential organizations as well as prominent religious figures and bolting Democratic leaders attacking Smith for one or more of the same reasons as were given by the secret order for its opposition to the standard-bearer of the Democratic party. Actively participating in the attempt to swing certain of the traditionally Democratic states to Hoover were, for example, such organizations as the Anti-Saloon League and the Woman's Christian Temperance Union and such individuals as Bishop James Cannon, Jr., of the Methodist Episcopal Church South; Dr. Hugh K. Walker, Moderator of the General Assembly of the Presbyterian Church; Dr. John Roach Straton of New York's Calvary Baptist Church; former Senator Robert L. Owen of Oklahoma; and Senator Furnifold McLendel Simmons of North Carolina.

And what is most difficult to determine is how an order that had recently been censured by the American public for its excesses, an order that had recently lost its formidable political potency, an order that had recently experienced a drop in membership from over 4,000,000 to a few hundred thousand, in short, an order that was about to collapse, could possibly play a decisive role in the presidential election of 1928. If the Invisible Empire, Knights of the Ku Klux Klan was indeed a major factor in the desertion of almost half the "Solid South" to the Republican candidate, then it was not the substance but the spirit of the secret fraternity — that nebulous and elusive quality — that made it so.

CHAPTER VIII

DISREPUTE AND DECLINE

At the end of 1928 the Ku Klux Klan did not expire; it merely laid itself down to recover from two blows: a sharp loss of membership as a result of popular disrepute at the height of its career, and exhaustion of its rapidly diminishing energies in its opposition to Alfred E. Smith's bid for the presidency. The Klan was never to regain the numerical strength or influence it had before 1928.

Interestingly enough, it was the Klansmen outside the borders of Dixie who during the 1930's tried to keep the fraternity from perishing. Throughout the decade of depression Knights in the North preserved ritual and customs via colorful ceremonies in lonely fields, blazing crosses on mountain tops, and grim parades.

In September, 1930, in Peekskill, New York, in the southeastern part of the state, a field day was attended by 500 hooded and robed Klansmen from New York, New Jersey, Massachusetts, and Pennsylvania. Activities included a military drill, fireworks, and the burning of a great "K" on a nearby hillside. The following July another field day was held in the same town. Highlighting this affair was an address by the Grand Klokard of the Realm of New York, M. D. L. Van Over.

A thousand members of the Klan, about one-fourth of them in regalia, gathered just outside of Somerville, New Jersey, in 1933, to participate in an Easter sunrise service in the glow of a fiery cross. Two years later, again near Somerville, 1,000 Knights assembled for the same purpose.

Members of the order held a three-day outdoor convention in Peekskill in September, 1936. In their first public appearance in that area in five years, the hooded and robed Klansmen conducted an initiation ceremony, participated in athletic contests, listened to speeches by their leaders, and set fire to a cross twenty feet high.

On the evening of October 1, 1937, the newest appointee to the Supreme Court, former Senator Hugo L. Black of Alabama, made a radio address to the nation in order to reply to charges levelled against him of membership in the Klan. This touched off a spate of fiery crosses in the North. In Worcester, Massachusetts; in Marlboro, fifteen miles to the northeast; in Hyde Park, New York, near President Franklin D. Roosevelt's estate; in Mountain Lakes, New Jersey, not too far from Newark, the night was momentarily ablaze with that symbol which was everywhere and immediately associated with the secret order. It should be noted that in each of these areas it was generally believed that the local Klan had already been dissolved. Consequently, the crosses could have been burned by individuals not belonging to the fraternity. However, the setting fire to a cross in the resort town of Mattituck, Long Island, in the summer of 1939, undoubtedly was the work of Klansmen; near the particular cross was a sign that meant business: "Jews are not wanted in Mattituck — K.K.K."

As for parading, Knights in regalia filed, for example, down the streets of Freeport, Long Island, in July, 1930; nearby Valley Stream, in September, 1931; Freeport again, in September, 1933. Sometimes the desire to march went unfulfilled because of opposition from community officials. In May, 1930, Klansmen from three counties in southeastern New York — Westchester, Putnam, and Rockland — filed application with the Board of Trustees of Mt. Kisco for permission to take part in the town's Memorial Day Parade. The board handed down a negative decision after the Memorial Day Committee along with twelve civic and fraternal organizations in the area requested that the Klan be barred from taking part in the march. In the fall of 1937 Kleagle William E. Cahill, after calling upon the city manager of Toledo, Ohio, in regard to a proposed tri-state parade of the Klan in that city, was told promptly that under no circumstances would a permit be issued for a parade of hooded and robed persons.

As in the 1920's, the practice of physically disciplining a wrongdoer (either real or imagined) was more prevalent among the Klansmen of the South than among those of other sections of the country. Following are some illustrations of the secret order's participation in "night-riding." In March, 1935, the manager of a hotel in St. Petersburg, Florida, Robert M. Cargell, was seized by five men, one of whom was the local Kleagle, and driven to a deserted spot, where he was horribly mutilated with a knife. In November, 1937, about 175 hooded and robed Klansmen swooped down on the La Paloma night club in Miami, Florida, where they struck entertainers and waiters, smashed furniture, compelled patrons to leave, and ordered the place closed. In the summer of 1939 two residents of suburban Atlanta, Georgia, were taken to a garbage dump where they were beaten for "immorality." That fall, in nearby Decatur, a white proprietor of a movie theater for Negroes was flogged by the local Klan because it did not like his business operation. During the Christmas season of 1939 a garage mechanic was dragged from his home in Anderson, South Carolina, in the middle of the night and mercilessly whipped because, his abductors said, he had slapped a child. On March 2, 1940, a young man and girl from Atlanta, who were alleged to have been violating the local Klan's conception of sexual morality, were found beaten to death in a parked car in a local lovers' lane. Less than a week later another resident of the city, a barber by the name of Ike Gaston, was visited by hooded men who killed him with a long cleated belt that was subsequently proved to have been made by an avowed Klansman.

Two conclusions that have been presented previously in this study regarding Klan violence bear restating at this point. Since the individuals committing the outrages were hidden behind Klan regalia, they could just as easily have not been members of the secret fraternity; if the men who engaged in these offenses were Klansmen, they could have been taking action without first obtaining the consent of the local chapter as a whole.

The activities engaged in by the Klan during the 1930's, such as conducting a ritual in a field outside of town, setting a huge cross ablaze, parading silently down the street, or taking punitive measures against wrongdoers could never check the longing of Knights to see their fraternity become once again a conspicuous power in American politics. The longing was never to be satisfied.

This does not mean, however, that in the years after 1928 the Klan never popped up in a political setting. Alabama is a good case in point. With his rabid attacks upon Alfred E. Smith before groups of Klansmen during the 1928 presidential campaign, Senator J. Thomas Heflin influenced 120,000 of the state's traditionally Democratic voters to cast their ballots for Herbert Hoover in November.[1] Only because of exhaustive toil on the part of Alabama's Democratic party organization was Smith able to carry this commonwealth of the "Solid South" —and by merely 7,000 votes. Heflin's term was to expire in 1931. When he announced his intention of entering the 1930 Democratic senatorial primary, the party avenged itself. The State Democratic Committee decreed that only candidates who had actively supported Smith in the election of 1928 could run on the Democratic ticket. Because he was barred from the primary, Heflin hoped to discomfit the party. In order to accomplish this, he accepted both Klan and Republican aid. An alliance of the bolting Heflin, the by then discredited Knights, and the loathed Republicans could do no other than to consolidate the Democratic party. John H. Bankhead, a corporation lawyer and coal mine operator, won the race for the Democratic nomination for the senatorship. In Alabama this was, of course, tantamount to victory in the general election to follow.

When Hugo L. Black vacated his legislative seat in 1937 to settle down on the judicial bench, Heflin struggled to occupy the former. In the special Democratic senatorial primary held on January 4, 1938, Lister Hill, Representative from the Second Congressional District of Alabama, defeated Heflin, who had been permitted once again to run on the ticket, by polling almost twice as many votes. The *New York Times* reflected the viewpoint of most newspapers when it wrote of this nearly two-to-one victory as follows: "Although the principles and loyalties for which Mr. Hill stood and his own personal effectiveness as a public man may be credited with the bulk of the support given him, the decisive factor in his victory was obviously Heflinism, an unwillingness on the part of many voters to identify themselves or their State again with the racial and religious hatred and the Ku Kluxery for which former Senator Heflin ... stands in national sight." Heflin's downfall was complete; he was never again to hold public office.

As for the Upper South, in the Maryland state election of 1938 the religious issue played an important part. The voters were swamped with anonymous letters attacking the Catholicism of the three top candidates on the Democratic ticket, including Attorney-General Herbert R. O'Conor, who was running for the governorship. Widely circulated was *The American Protestant*, a newspaper published in Washington, D. C., containing appeals to vote against the Catholic office-seekers. The journal also declared frantically that out of forty-two candidates in the city of Baltimore for the state Senate and House of Delegates, more than three-fourths were Catholics. In 1928 the Klan in Maryland had actively opposed Alfred E. Smith's presidential candidacy. It was believed by numerous observers ten years later that the secret order was just as involved in politics in 1938, for the anti-Catholic campaign literature that was being circulated in that year was more than coincidentally similar to that issued by the Klan in Maryland in the past.

In New York City one of those entered in the September, 1938, open primary in Kings County, which is coextensive with the Borough of Brooklyn, was Louis Waldman. As the American Labor party candidate for a judgeship, Waldman announced that the Klan had flooded the area with appeals to the people to vote against him. Seeking office in a political district having an electorate composed quite largely of Jews, Catholics, Negroes, and the foreign-born, Waldman attempted to make the most of the hostility of the Klan, a hostility which, of course, could not have been damaging in a place such as Brooklyn. "I welcome the opposition of the K.K.K.," he said. "Their Americanism isn't mine, and my principles and ideals are not theirs." Waldman was, however, not victorious in the primary.

During the 1920's a great number of officeholders, in both the North and the South, either allied themselves, or flirted, with the Klan. In the 1930's few public officials dared to be friendly toward the order. Three southern states—South Carolina, Georgia, and Florida—composed a contiguous territory in which this was not the case. By 1939, for example: in Greenville, South Carolina, nearly every member of the police force was conceded to be a Klansman; the acting sheriff of Anderson County, South Carolina, which is situated in the northwestern part of the state, was an avowed Knight; three deputy sheriffs of Fulton County, Georgia, admitted to membership in the secret fraternity; in Orlando, Florida, Klan parades were frequently honored by an escort of police; in Tampa and Miami, city officials, both elected and appointed, were on intimate terms with representatives of the order.

In the decade and a half following 1928 there kept cropping up against well-known political figures accusations of former Klan affiliation. In each instance the secret order itself played a quite passive role. The most celebrated case is the one that "broke" in 1937. On August 12 of that year, a message from President Franklin D. Roosevelt was delivered to the Senate. It read: "I nominate [Senator] Hugo L. Black of Alabama to be an Associate Justice of the Supreme Court of the United States." To a request made for unanimous consent to consider the message at once, there was objection, shattering a custom of the Upper House to confirm without reference to committee the nomination of any of its members to any office. A hearing had to be held; Black was, in the end, approved by the Senate. On October 4, the Alabaman took his place on the bench. His first official act as an Associate Justice was to hear motions contesting his right to the office. Demands were made that the House of Representatives impeach Justice Black and that the Senate try and convict him. All this over current rumors linking Black with the Invisible Empire, Knights of the Ku Klux Klan.

The full case against Black was not made known until after the Senate had confirmed his nomination. The facts were set forth in a series of six articles written by Ray Sprigle and published in the

Pittsburgh Post-Gazette beginning September 13, 1937.[2] Using as evidence attestations by affidavit of former Knights who were witnesses to certain Klan functions, photostatic reproductions of official and hitherto secret Klan records, and stenographic notes taken by A. B. Hale, a then official reporter of the order, Sprigle related the following regarding the newly-appointed Justice: He had joined the Robert E. Lee Klan No. 1, Invisible Empire, Knights of the Ku Klux Klan, in Birmingham on September 11, 1923. On July 9, 1925, before beginning his race for the Democratic nomination for the United States senatorship, he formally resigned from the order upon the suggestion of Klan officials, so that he could campaign with all the advantages of Klan support but without any of the disadvantages of having to admit to Klan membership if challenged on that score during the 1926 primary. On September 2, 1926, after gaining the nomination,[3] which is tantamount to winning the election in Democratic Alabama, Black was welcomed back to the secret fraternity at a "Klorero" (state meeting) in Birmingham, at which time he received a gold "grand passport" (life membership card) in the Klan.

In attendance at the Klorero were about 2,000 Knights, including Imperial Wizard Evans, Grand Dragon James Esdale of the Realm of Alabama, Great Titans from three Provinces, and Exalted Cyclopses from fifty local Klans. After some minutes of good-humored allusions by Klan officials to Black's success in the recently held primary, the Senator-nominate was brought to the speaker's stand amid great applause to be given the gold-engraved certificate of life membership in the secret fraternity. In his speech accepting the grand passport, Black expressed his full sympathy with the principles of the Klan, and asked for the counsel of the organization when he assumed his new political post. As to his winning the senatorial nomination, he attributed it to Klan backing. "I do not feel that it would be out of place to state to you here on this occasion that I know that without the support of the members of this organization I would have not been called ... [as so introduced] the 'Junior Senator from Alabama.'"

Two and a half weeks after the initial Sprigle article appeared Black made his first and only comment on the charge levelled against him of Klan affiliation. On the evening of October 1, 1937, he delivered a short address over the radio, in which he said:

"... I joined the Ku Klux Klan about fifteen years ago ... I later resigned. I never re-joined. What appeared then or what appears now on the records of the organization I do not know.

"I never have considered and I do not now consider the unsolicited card given to me shortly after my nomination to the Senate as a membership of any kind in the Ku Klux Klan. I never used it. I did not even keep it."

When the Justice bid goodnight to those who had been listening to him, he ended an episode that <u>was</u> indeed unique in the history of American political life.[4]

Hugo L. Black was not the only politician of Alabama honored at the Klorero in Birmingham on September 2, 1926. According to the Sprigle articles, at this state meeting of the Invisible Empire, Colonel Bibb Graves of Montgomery,[5] the then Democratic nominee for the governorship, was also presented with a grand passport, which he accepted with a short address expressing gratitude for the Klan's support in the recently held primary,[6] pledging loyalty to Klan principles, and requesting Klan advice in the discharge of his new public duties. The Governor-nominate's peroration is of especial interest: " ... every real enemy of Klancraft throughout the State and this country would really delight in seeing a Cyclops-Governor the greatest failure in American history. The Klan is on trial; it is not Bibb Graves but it is the Ku Klux Klan that stands on trial, not only in Alabama but throughout America."[7]

At the height of the Black affair in 1937 Graves, by then serving a second term as Governor of Alabama, in an interview with a *New York Times* reporter, admitted attending, as a Knight, the Klorero on September 2, 1926. He admitted, also, receiving on that occasion what he referred to as "some kind of badge," but added that he had never attached any great importance to that award. Graves pooh-poohed the suggestion by the newspaperman that he still had the status of a Knight in view of the nature of the grand passport as a symbol of life membership. He emphasized that when he became Governor in 1927, he disassociated himself from the order, not by writing a letter of resignation, but by merely "dropping out" through the non-payment of dues and the non-attendance of meetings.

But to other cases. In August, 1938, while he was seeking a second term as Senator from California, William G. McAdoo was charged with holding life membership in the Klan. The accusation was made by Peirson Hall, campaign manager for McAdoo's Republican opponent for the senatorship, Sheridan Downey. In Hall's possession was the grand passport allegedly given McAdoo by the secret fraternity; how he himself obtained possession of the life membership card Hall would not say. Dog-eared and hardly decipherable, the gold-engraved certificate read:

"To All Exalted Cyclops, Greetings:

"The bearer, Kl. William G. McAdoo, whose signature and present address is on the [the printing is here obliterated], is a citizen of the Invisible Empire, and to him is given this Imperial Passport that he may travel throughout our beneficent domain and grant and have the fervent fellowship of Klansmen. By this authority you will pass him through the portals of your Klaverns to meet with Klansmen in Konklave assembled.

"Signed and sealed this twenty-ninth day of February, 1924, by His Lordship, H. W. Evans, Imperial Wizard and Imperial Cyclops."

To Hall's accusation McAdoo replied that any statement that he was or ever had been a member of the Klan was "utterly and wantonly false." As to the grand passport specifically, the Californian said, "Any purported certificate issued to me by the Klan must be a forgery, as I have never had any such certificate and have never seen one." Contacted in Atlanta, where the Klan had re-established its national headquarters after having transferred them to Washington, D. C., in 1928, Imperial Wizard Evans told the press that he had no knowledge of McAdoo's ever having been a Knight, and that he, as the head of the order, had never signed a life membership card for the politician. That McAdoo failed to be re-elected to the Upper House in 1938 is a matter of public record; that the charge of Klan affiliation was responsible for the defeat is not.

Two aspects of the affair must be brought to light. First, before becoming chief strategist for Senator McAdoo's political enemy, Hall had tried unsuccessfully to obtain a quite necessary recommendation from the Senator for reappointment as United States Attorney. Second, the internal evidence of the alleged grand passport forces the serious student of the Klan to deem it non-genuine. No Knight would ever omit the "l" in the first syllable of the word "Klonklave," or refer to the Imperial Wizard as "His Lordship" or "Imperial Cyclops."

In June, 1944, the Republican national committeeman from Indiana was denounced by a member of his own party as having been an active Klansman in the 1920's under Grand Dragon David Curtis Stephenson of the Realm of Indiana. The accused was Robert W. Lyons, a millionaire lawyer and chain-store lobbyist. After being subjected to two weeks of bitter criticism, against which he did not choose to defend himself, Lyons resigned from his political post.

That fall two candidates for public office were charged with former membership in the Klan. The first one admitted to it; he happened to be defeated. On October 23, 1944, the Democratic nominee for the

House of Representatives from the Fifteenth Congressional District of California, Hal Styles, announced that he had joined the Klan in 1926, but that four years later he purged himself by writing a series of articles exposing the order and holding it up to public condemnation. Styles, however, did not remain on the defensive. He asserted that his Republican opponent, out of desperation for office, finally had had to resort to waging a smear campaign.

The second candidate denied the charge of past membership in the secret fraternity; he was elected. On October 26, 1944, at a press conference held in Peoria, Illinois, the Democratic nominee for the vice-presidency, Senator Harry S. Truman of Missouri, commented in detail on the story currently being circulated that he was a former Klansman. After he dismissed the account as a "lie" which had been "nailed" in 1922, when he successfully ran for the judgeship of the County Court for the Eastern District of Jackson, Missouri, Truman went on to emphasize that the order had always fought him in his home state. At a meeting of the Grand Lodge of Masons in September, 1921, in St. Louis, he had worked in behalf of a resolution to expel any lodge member who had joined the Klan, he added. The Senator asserted that he had never attended a Klan gathering. "If I had shown up at a meeting," he quipped, "the Klan would have pulled me apart."

The most the secret fraternity was capable of doing politically during the 1930's was to prevent, ever so often, Negroes in southern communities from exercizing the franchise. For example, in Starke, Florida, near the Georgia border, on the night before the municipal election of September 13, 1938, hooded and robed Klansmen visited the Negro section of town, where they burned two crosses and left notes warning the colored population to "stay out of Bradford County politics or take the consequences." In Miami, on the night before the Democratic primary of May 2, 1939, Knights in regalia filled about fifty automobiles, the license plates of which were shielded, and drove through the Negro section of the city, tossing out cards marked "K. K. K." in red and bearing the legend: "Respectable Negro citizens are not voting tomorrow. Niggers stay away from the polls." Before the Klansmen withdrew, they had set fire to twenty-five crosses along the railroad tracks.

There is a difference between the success of Klan intimidation of the Negro electorate in the 1920's and that in the 1930's that begs for emphasis. In the latter decade the demonstrations of the secret order failed to prevent the Negro community as a whole from showing up at the polls. As a matter of fact, in the Miami Democratic primary of

May 2, 1939, the colored population ignored the warning issued by the Klan to cast a record vote.

Initiation ceremonies, field days, Easter sunrise services, setting crosses ablaze, parades, "night-riding," intimidation of the Negro electorate—these things kept the Klan merely alive during the 1930's. Imperial Wizard Evans, now somewhat jowlier and a great deal paunchier, must have racked his brains over the proper approach to be used in order to regain for his fraternity the tremendous influence, both social and political, that it had enjoyed in the previous decade. Times do change! To make a comeback perhaps it was necessary to add to the original creed of the secret order. In the early summer of 1934 Evans took that step when he announced:

"Public-spirited people, klansmen and non-members alike, realize that this nation is in great danger. Because of its record of heroic achievement, the Klan has been called upon by them to mobilize . . .

"Klansmen in action, competent and courageous, will lead the American people to see that individual liberty and Constitutional Government shall not perish and that this nation be no longer the victim of alien propaganda."

What was the substance of the alien propaganda against which a revived Invisible Empire, Knights of the Ku Klux Klan was to be a bulwark? It was Communism. Taking its place in the mid-1930's alongside the established beliefs of the fraternity—white supremacy, anti-Semitism, anti-foreign-bornism, anti-Catholicism, "pure" Americanism, Protestantism and strict morality—was the new tenet of anti-Communism.

A post-World War II leader of the Klan, Dr. Samuel J. Green, was wont to iterate that it was his order which first "discovered" Communism in the United States and which first assailed it—in the year 1929. "Congressmen laughed at us from the start," he once chided. As to historicity, Green's contention leaves everything to be desired. Be that as it may, from the very beginning of the 1930's Klansmen despised American Communists because of their efforts to court Negroes with proffers of economic advancement and racial equality. In March, 1931, fourteen armed Knights abducted and flogged two Communist organizers in Dallas, Texas, for making speeches against Jim Crow laws and the widespread lynching of Negroes. In downtown Birmingham, Alabama, on a late afternoon in November, 1932, Negroes were showered by paper pamphlets tossed from a building by members of the local Klan. The message read: "Negroes of Birmingham, the Klan is watching you. Tell the Communists to get out of town.

They mean only trouble for you, for Alabama is a good place for good Negroes and a bad place for Negroes who believe in racial equality. Report Communistic activities to the Ku Klux Klan, Box 661, Birmingham."

In the next few years Klan leaders consciously de-emphasized the anti-Negroism, anti-Semitism, anti-foreign-bornism, and anti-Catholicism of their fraternity. And it was made quite clear to the nation that the new crusade of the organization was aimed at Communism. Klan oratory in New York illustrates well the point. On September 4, 1933, the order ended a three-day convention on a vacant lot in Freeport, Long Island, with platform appearances of hooded and robed speakers expounding on the importance of Klan success in arousing the American people to the menace of Communism. The following September, after three years of inactivity, the local chapter in Westchester County held a reorganization meeting. A Kleagle who had arrived in an automobile bearing a Rhode Island license plate told his fellow Knights: "The Klan is needed now, particularly in this section of the country, so that we can give back to the American people the fundamental rights conveyed by the Constitution. Communism must be stamped out. The New Deal has become communistic and I feel certain that the American public will rise in protest and soundly defeat President Roosevelt at the next general election."

Speaking to about 75 of his charges for more than an hour on September 5, 1936, the Grand Dragon of the Realm of New York, H. W. Garing, asserted repeatedly that their order was not in the least anti-Negro, anti-Catholic, or anti-Semitic, but was in every respect anti-Communistic.

In the Middle West a drive was under way in the fall of 1937 to revive the Klan in the states of Ohio, Indiana, and Michigan. As part of the program for resuscitation, letters were sent out by Kleagles summoning back all former Knights. Across the bottom of these epistles were five words: "Communism Will Not Be Tolerated."

The unprecedented growth during the 1920's of various mass production enterprises, such as the automobile industry, had made it necessary for skilled and unskilled workers to toil under the same roof. The latter were denied membership in the American Federation of Labor which was limited to skilled workers in a particular trade. When, in 1935, certain labor leaders, led by John L. Lewis of the United Mine Workers, failed to convince the American Federation of Labor that unskilled workers should be permitted to join its ranks, ten unions within the federation formed the Committee for Industrial Organization.

Its goal was to organize all workers in the mass production industries. Three years later the Committee for Industrial Organization completely severed itself from the American Federation of Labor, changing its title to the Congress of Industrial Organizations.

The heads of the Committee for Industrial Organization quickly discovered that Communists would be quite helpful in their attempt to organize the mass production industries. Of course, labor leaders had from the very beginning decided merely to "use" the Communists, and they dropped them just as soon as Communist tactics were deemed no longer necessary.[8] The Committee for Industrial Organization was thus grist for the Klan mill.

While Akron, Ohio, was experiencing a period of anxiety in 1936 due to a "sit-down"strike in the local B. F. Goodrich tire plant, Kleagles successfully "worked" the city for new members. Even after the industrial dispute was resolved with the return to work of 10,000 employees in late September, Akron's labor relations were to remain unsettled, for the newly reactivated local Klan began a crusade against Communism, which was in reality directed against labor unions in general and the Committee for Industrial Organization in particular.

In the early summer of 1937 Imperial Wizard Evans moved his offices from rural Roswell Road, about ten miles outside of Atlanta, to the heart of the city. It is strongly noncoincidental that Evans' change of headquarters took place at the same time that the Steel Workers Organizing Committee and the Textile Workers Organizing Committee, both affiliates of the Committee for Industrial Organization, began their joint campaigns of unionizing laborers in the southeastern part of the nation. Soon after the Texile Workers Organizing Committee started operations, its organizers in Chattanooga, Tennessee, Columbus, Georgia, and other smaller southern cities, found crosses burning in the night in the immediate vicinity of their residences. In Greenville, South Carolina, an active center of the textile industry, within a week after the Textile Workers Organizing Committee began its campaign, there appeared tacked onto telephone poles and billboards hundreds of cards carrying this message:

> "C. I. O. is Communism
> Communism
> Will Not Be Tolerated
> Ku Klux Klan
> Rides Again"

On July 11, 1937, the Imperial Wizard declared that the Committee for Industrial Organization was "infested" with Communists. Referring to the current labor strife in the nation, Evans said, "The Klan will not sit idly by and allow the C. I. O. to destroy our social order, nor shall the C. I. O. flout law and promote social disorder without swift punishment." Two weeks later an announcement was issued from Evans' headquarters that the Klan would hold a series of demonstrations throughout the nation as a protest against "alien labor agitation." The first of these public displays took place in Atlanta on July 31, 1937, when Klansmen living in or near that city paraded in full regalia behind a fiery cross.

In 1937, while on a murder trial assignment in Tampa, Florida, a New York Times correspondent took time out to talk to many representative inhabitants of the area regarding the part the Klan had played in southern life. One of those interviewed was a middle-aged successful attorney in Bartow, forty miles southeast of Tampa, who took vehement issue with what he considered to be the standard thinking in the North on the Klan—that the order would never again be an active, effective one. Maintaining that his views were those of the great majority of the substantial citizens of southern small towns, the lawyer said, "Down here, we, who have heard John L. Lewis' promise to unionize all labor, know the Klan will be in the spotlight for a long time to come. When the C. I. O. comes here, as it promises to do, the Klan will start up all over again."

The foresight of the southern small town lawyer and the hindsight of organizers for the Congress of Industrial Organizations two years later were completely compatible. Delegates to the convention of the Texile Workers Union of America, in Philadelphia, in May, 1939 were told by organizers that a primary reason why the "No. 1 task" of full and complete unionization of all southern textile workers was still unfinished was the vicious hostility of a revived Klan.

The secret fraternity, however, was not able to resuscitate during the mid-1930's—not even as the clamorously self-advertised bulwark against Communism and the unionization of the mass production industries by leftist labor leaders. The reason appears to be twofold. First, during the depression years whatever money a man was able to acquire was used for the basic necessities of life. One's wife and children had to be provided with some food, some clothing, some kind of shelter. Nothing was left over to accumulate into $10 for the Klectoken or into $5 for the regalia, let alone into the sum demanded regularly by the local chapter as dues. In early 1934 the Memphis

Commercial-Appeal editorialized that although the Klan prospered during the post-World War I period of "economic abandon," values had changed since then. "Even fraternities of ancient establishment have found it difficult to survive. 'Jiners' have been conspicuous by their absence since 1929. They'll still be absent when the hooded Atlantans try to meet again in the groves." The years were to prove right this southern newspaper.

Second, other organizations came into being during the mid-1930's which had ideologies that immediately captured the allegiance of millions of Americans who would ordinarily have been excellent prospects for the Kleagle. Dr. Francis E. Townsend of California launched the Old Age Revolving Pension plan to return the nation to general prosperity by paying $200 per month to every individual over sixty years old with the requirement that the entire sum be spent before the next $200 was obtained. In 1935, the Pacific coast physician claimed 5,000,000 followers. In the spring of that year Senator Huey P. Long of Louisiana announced his Share the Wealth program which involved the federal government's guaranteeing every family in the nation an annual income of at least $5,000. Clubs were organized by the Senator in many states to work actively in behalf of his scheme. Then there were the new "hate" groups, such as William Dudley Pelley's Silver Shirt Legion of America, and the Rev. Gerald L. K. Smith's Committee of One Million.

On January 16, 1939, Imperial Wizard Evans astounded the country by accepting the invitation of Bishop Gerald P. O'Hara of the Savannah-Atlanta Catholic Diocese to attend the dedication ceremonies for Atlanta's new Cathedral of Christ the King. (The edifice was built on the site of the first national Klan headquarters. After the Klan had established a new headquarters in Washington, D. C., in 1928, it sold the property to an insurance company, which in turn sold it to the Diocese.) Further, Evans consented to appearance in the press of a photograph of himself standing cordially next to Bishop O'Hara and Denis Cardinal Dougherty of Philadelphia, who was also in attendance at the dedication ceremonies for the cathedral. A leading Methodist minister in Atlanta, the Rev. Walter Holcomb, surely spoke for millions of Americans when he characterized the entire incident as "one of the greatest triumphs over intolerance that I have ever seen."

Evans' deed is the most notable illustration of the Klan's abandonment, whether actual or ostensible, of religio-racial antipathies for the sake of its new crusade against Communism and the Committee for Industrial Organization. The actions of the Imperial Wizard of the

Ku Klux Klan were always to be given proper respect throughout each and every division of the Invisible Empire. Evans discovered, however, that while he had been in attendance at the dedication ceremonies for the cathedral, he had been acting for himself, not for Klansmen throughout the nation. Whether his decision to publicly congregate with members of the Catholic hierarchy had stemmed from sincerity or artfulness made little or no difference; his action had been too extreme for Klandom.

A few months later, on June 10, at a Klonvokation in Atlanta attended by Knights from thirty states, Evans relinquished the post he had held for nearly two decades. He stoutly denied that there was any internal dissension in the order over policy in general or over his attendance at the dedication ceremonies in particular; he maintained that at the time he had been re-elected Imperial Wizard in 1935, he had decided that he would not be a candidate to succeed himself.

Acceding to the Imperial Wizardship was James A. Colescott, a stocky, bespectacled forty-two year old former veterinarian from Terre Haute, Indiana.° Active in the secret order since 1923, Dr. Colescott had served it as Grand Dragon of the Realm of Ohio, later as liaison officer between national headquarters and local Klans in Pennsylvania, Indiana, Michigan, Kentucky, and Texas, and for the past two years as Evans' personal and chief assistant in Atlanta.

In his first public announcement after taking office, Colescott promised that the interests of the "native-born, white, Protestant gentile" population of the country would be promoted by an "administration of action." The new Imperial Wizard tried to keep his troth with his fellow Knights. Under Colescott the anti-Negroism, anti-Semitism anti-foreign-bornism, and anti-Catholicism of the twentieth century Klan were no longer soft-pedaled; the original creed of the order was ardently reaffirmed.

As for an "administration of action," during Colescott's first half dozen months as head of the Invisible Empire, a record of considerable growth and development was established. Membership lists of the 1920's were retrieved from the files and used as a basis for intensive recruitment operations. Kleagles were trained in the South during the winter of 1939-1940 to "work" the Middle West the following spring. The Imperial Wizard himself canvassed the Atlantic coast for new Knights. Crosses were set ablaze in, for example, Yonkers, New York; Roselle, New Jersey, south of Newark; Uniontown, Pennsylvania; Baltimore, Maryland; Muncie, Indiana; Ferndale, Michigan, just outside of Detroit; and in several towns in Georgia, Florida, and California.

Local Klans were set up in such important cities as Providence, Rhode Island; Schenectady, New York; Jersey City, New Jersey; Philadelphia, Pennsylvania; Cincinnati, Ohio; Urbana, Illinois; and Kansas City, Missouri. The factory making the official Klan regalia speeded up production of the costume, which was reduced from the long established original price of $5 to $3. National Klan headquarters was refurbished and enlarged.

Obviously anticipating widespread antipathy toward a reactivated Klan, the Imperial Wizard on April 17, 1940, issued an edict forbidding the wearing of the hood at any time and restricting the burning of crosses to formal ceremonies.

Colescott boasted that during the first year of his rule Klan membership increased by 50 per cent, that by the summer of 1940 there were 500,000 Knights in thirty-nine states. Estimates by contemporary reporters of the organization, however, put membership closer to 200,000. Whatever the numerical strength of the Klan was in 1940, it can be said with certainty that two out of every three Knights was a Southerner.

Colescott's program of expansion was abruptly and decisively cut short by a force quite outside his reach—World War II. Through two separate acts, the first shortly before, and the second soon after, American entry into the war, the Klan hoped to prove to the nation its basic patriotism. In October, 1941, it was reported that the fraternity was printing the slogan "Buy a Share in America—Buy Savings Bonds" on the application forms it sent to prospective members. In January, 1942, it was announced from national headquarters that "in keeping with its policy of Americanism," the order had withdrawn from circulation after the declaration of war against Japan, "all" its pamphlets "of a controversial nature."

Then, Klan activity virtually ceased. From 1942 to 1945, those few Americans who for one reason or another happened to be interested in news of the secret order searched their daily papers fruitlessly for months at a time for an article on, or a report of, the Klan; those many Americans who happened not to be interested read in their daily papers of world-wide hostilities and their concomitant miseries—and quickly forgot about the Klan.

Chapter IX

A SPLINTERED BODY

In November, 1944, Dr. H. Scudder Mekeel, Associate Professor of Anthropology at the University of Wisconsin, warned those gathered before him for the annual meeting of the National Committee for Mental Hygiene that there was a real possibility that the conclusion of the war currently being waged against Germany and Japan would be followed by a revival "in full force" of the Ku Klux Klan.

Seven months before Mekeel made his remarks, the secret order had officially dissolved itself. Being hounded by the Bureau of Internal Revenue for not having paid past taxes amounting to $685,305, the Klan held a Klonvokation in Atlanta, Georgia, on April 23, 1944, at which the hierarchy of Knights assembled "repealed all decrees, vacated all offices, voided all charters, and relieved every klansman of any obligation whatever." Imperial Wizard Colescott was consequently released from the post he had held for a half dozen years. It was thus hoped that any entanglement with the federal government over tax suits would be avoided.

But this did not mean the dissolution of the Klan in actuality. At the same Klonvokation it was decided to establish an "informal, unincorporated" alliance of the local chapters of the fraternity operating in the state of Georgia. Chosen to lead the newly organized Association of Georgia Klans with the title of Grand Dragon was Dr. Samuel J. Green, a toothbrush-mustachioed, bespectacled fifty-four year old obstetrician from Atlanta. The physician had been an active Knight since 1922.[1] While disclaiming a legal relationship between the Invisible Empire, Knights of the Ku Klux Klan and the Association of Georgia Klans, Dr. Green made no secret that the latter would perpetuate the philosophy, ritual, and methods of operation of its inactive forebear.

Associate Professor Mekeel had been perceptive. Retired from sight during World War II, the Klan appeared on the American scene soon after hostilities ceased. Frequently, from the fall of 1945 to the spring of 1946, huge fiery crosses on top of Stone Mountain, outside of Atlanta, lighted up the night. It was here on May 9, 1946, that the secret fraternity conducted its first large postwar initiation ceremony.

The public had been invited through advertisements in the press. The approximately 2,000 who responded saw more than 200 individuals kneel before Grand Dragon Green to take a sacred oath of allegiance to the order. Exulted Green, "We are revived."

The membership of the Klan in Georgia was estimated in the middle of 1946 to be between 40,000 and 50,000, about half of which was centered in Atlanta. By 1949 the fraternity had achieved its goal of an active local Klan in each of the 159 counties of the state. Green announced that he was receiving from all over the nation requests for the formation of chapters, usually from groups with a starting strength of 100.

Very quickly the revived fraternity gained political influence in Georgia. In 1946, in his bid for a fourth term as Governor of the Empire State of the South, Eugene Talmadge publicly declared he would welcome along with the support of all other white inhabitants the backing of Klansmen. After the Democratic gubernatorial primary of July 17, Grand Dragon Green was wont to boast that by the most intensive activity the order had contributed 100,000 votes to Talmadge, thus assuring him the nomination of his party. In solidly Democratic Georgia, Talmadge, of course, went on to victory over his Republican opponent in the general election that followed. Before he could take office, however, he died. In 1949 his son Herman acceded to the governorship. In June of that year Green announced that he was a member of Governor Herman Talmadge's personal staff. In Green's office in Atlanta a newspaper reporter had indeed spotted what appeared to be a framed commission designating Green as a lieutenant colonel and aide-de-camp to the Governor and bearing Talmadge's name. When the Chief Executive was asked whether the Grand Dragon was a staff member, he replied simply, "I don't know."

In a host of southern cities outside the boundaries of Georgia, including Knoxville, Tennessee, Key West, Florida, and Birmingham, Alabama, Knights were holding regular meetings. In Birmingham, for example, there were four chapters of the Klan, with a total membership of 1,000. In and around that city on a single spring night in 1946 eight crosses were set ablaze.

The Klan was making headway in the North, too. On March 21, 1946, fiery crosses appeared in Flint, Michigan, after it was announced that a Negro would be a candidate for a municipal post. Some weeks later crosses were burned near the home of a Negro in Los Angeles, California, in a field north of that city, and in front of a house belonging to a Jewish fraternity on the campus of the University of Southern

California. In the fall of 1946, the King Kleagle of Indiana, Harold Overton, told the press that the Klan in the Hoosier State had recruiters at work in sixty of the ninety-two counties, was processing 121,000 application forms, and was engaged in setting up its headquarters in Muncie.

Resurgence was met by resistance. The vast majority of Americans, including those south of the Mason-Dixon line, shuddered at the revival of the Klan. In the post-World War I period most individuals who were repelled by Klanism decided against voicing their feelings because of the real possibility of extremist counter-measures on the part of the powerful secret order. This was not the case after World War II. Vigorous opposition to the Klan came from many quarters—independent citizens acting in concert, veterans groups, church associations, and government bodies.

On September 14, 1946, leaders of the nation's Negroes meeting in Los Angeles started a campaign to acquire a million signatures on a petition to outlaw the Klan. Citizens of Macon, Georgia, who were very much concerned over periodic outbursts of Klan activity banded together in 1948 to agitate for the enactment of a municipal ordinance prohibiting the masking of one's face in public. In December, 1948, a cross was set ablaze in front of the home of Jere Moore, the anti-Klan editor of the *Milledgeville, Georgia Union Recorder*. After Moore retaliated with an editorial accusing the secret order of threatening freedom of the press, ten influential citizens of the town put up a $1,000 reward for the apprehension of the cross-burners.

At the closing session of a convention of the Jewish War Veterans in Liberty, New York, in June, 1946, a resolution was adopted condemning the Klan and requesting that the federal government determine to what extent the order was violating the law. Some months later those attending the annual convention of the New Jersey branch of the American Legion censured the secret fraternity and called upon the governor and his staff to do all in their power to prevent any such organization from operating in the Garden State. In 1949 Klan terrorism in Alabama aroused the wrath of American Legionnaires in that commonwealth to the extent that they officially determined to "put an end" to such lawlessness. Soon after, 500 militant members of the Georgia branch of the American Legion banded together to back up law enforcement in all matters pertaining to the Klan.

In the resistance to postwar Klanism various Protestant church organizations took a big lead. This, of course, did an immense amount of good for the anti-Klan movement, since Protestants were not expected to be as resolute in their opposition to the secret order as the racial, religious, or ethnic groups against which it railed. In the fall of 1947 the Presbyterian Synod of New York adopted a committee report deploring the revival of the fraternity. The following summer, Presbyterian leaders from all of the southern states meeting in Montreat, North Carolina, labeled Klanism "definitely akin to fascism" and called on the House of Representatives Committee on Un-American Activities to investigate the order.

Other church groups were not to be outdone by their Presbyterian brethren. The South Carolina Baptist Convention resolved to fight the Klan, calling it "an unnecessary organization totally at variance with our Christian and democratic way of life"; the association of Methodist ministers in Atlanta adopted a resolution denouncing the fraternity as a "cowardly anti-Christian mob."

In the late 1940's there were incidents of Knights in regalia interrupting church services in order to present the minister with an envelope containing money. Such Klan benevolence was quite common during the 1920's and went uncriticized officially by Protestant spokesmen in high position. This was not so two decades later. Dr. Hugh A. Brimm, Executive Secretary of the Social Service Commission of the Southern Baptist Convention, on January 28, 1949, requested all pastors in his denomination to do the following in case their services were interrupted by Klansmen bearing cash gifts:

"(1) Keep cool— no one should be afraid of cowards who won't show their faces.

"(2) Remember that superficial piety is hypocrisy before God and man. These men cannot wash the blood stains of lynched victims from their skirts by merely walking into a church with 'blood money.'

"(3) Refuse any gifts and invite them to stay only if they remove their masks. If they refuse to unhood themselves, then dismiss the service with a prayer for them that they might see the light of God's love for all men and themselves come to love all men."

The most telling blow to Klanism in the post-World War II period was delivered by government on all three levels—federal, state, and local. In the spring of 1946 an investigator for the House of Representatives Committee on Un-American Activities was to travel to Atlanta, Georgia, for an on-the-spot search into the resurgence of the Klan. It was suggested by one spokesman for the committee that the inquiry might be extended to California, where the order was periodically bestirring itself.

Soon after, Assistant Attorney-General T. Lamar Caudle announced that government agents were looking into reports that the German-American Bund was reviving and had recently formed an alliance with the Klan. To bolster his charge that the two organizations had collaborated prior to World War II, Caudle declared that he possessed documentary evidence to show the following: in 1937 a leader of the Bund said that his group was co-operating with the Klan, since the aims of the two were "similar in many ways"; in that same year the two bodies considered forming an anti-labor third party; on August 18, 1940, the Bund and the Klan held a joint outdoor rally at the former's Camp Nordland, situated in the northwestern part of New Jersey.

In May, 1946, after condemning the revived Klan, Attorney-General Tom C. Clark declared that all the laws at his command would be used to stamp out any organization that was steeped in bigotry. Some weeks later Clark revealed that the activities of the secret fraternity in seven states—Tennessee, Georgia, Florida, Mississippi, New York, Michigan, and California—were being examined by the Federal Bureau of Investigation to ascertain whether any federal laws were being broken. In December, 1947, the Klan was listed by the Attorney-General, along with ninety-five other groups, as being disloyal to the nation.

The representatives of state government eagerly took up the cudgels against the secret fraternity. As soon as the Attorney-General of California, Robert W. Kenney, had finished parading a throng of former Knights before Superior Judge Alfred A. Paonessa to prove his contention that the Klan "taught racial hatred through violence and intimidation," the jurist revoked the California charter of the order and denied it the right to obtain a new permit in that state. Paonessa's action was taken on May 21, 1946, in Los Angeles.

After California prohibited the Klan from operating within its boundaries, other states quickly did the same. On the application of New York's Attorney-General, State Supreme Court Justice Joseph A. Gavagan, in July, 1946, signed an order revoking the state charter of the Klan and dissolving the organization. Anyone who atempted to sustain the life of the secret fraternity in the Empire State faced a fine of $10,000 and imprisonment up to six months.

Later that summer Kentucky took legal action. The Attorney-General filed suit to have the Klan's corporate rights in the state revoked, charging that the fraternity persecuted certain citizens because of their racial or religious background, after which Judge William B. Ardery in Circuit Court in Frankfort, Franklin County, directed the clerk of the court to enter a default judgment restraining the Klan "from holding itself out in any way as a corporation duly authorized to do business in Kentucky."

Then New Jersey outlawed the order. The testimony submitted by Attorney-General Walter D. Van Riper stressed the "improper" objectives of the Klan and its past link with the German-American Bund. (Those Knights who had participated with members of the Bund in the joint meeting at Camp Nordland in 1940 were, Van Riper noted, New Jersey leaders of the Klan.) Sitting in Trenton on October 10, 1946, State Supreme Court Justice A. Dayton Oliphant ruled "inoperative" a perpetual charter granted the order by New Jersey in 1923.

The state charter granted the Klan in Wisconsin in 1925 was revoked in December, 1946, bu Judge Herman V. Sachtjen in Circuit Court in Madison, Dane County. Sachtjen announced that his ruling was based on findings that showed that the secret fraternity stood for principles which were contrary to the letter and spirit of both the state and federal constitutions.

On June 13, 1947, the Klan voluntarily surrendered its Georgia charter in Superior Court in Atlanta, Fulton County. The secret order acted thus only after the state had deleted from an original charter revocation suit charges of murder, flogging, and breach of the public peace. The amended suit that was filed declared only that the Klan had forfeited its charter privileges because it had been incorporated as a benevolent and eleemosynary organization, whereas actually it had operated for profit to itself and certain of its members. Governor M. E. Thompson declared himself in favor of prosecuting the suit against the Klan, but the credit for the revocation of the Georgia charter of the order went to former Governor Ellis Arnall, who in May, 1946, had directed the Attorney-General to begin proceedings to that end.[2]

In 1949 Alabama joined the other states in curbing the Klan. On June 28 of that year Governor James E. Folsom signed a bill prohibiting the wearing of masks in public and immediately announced that he would issue an executive order calling for rigid enforcement of the new law. The state legislature had given almost unanimous approval to the unmasking bill. On June 17 the Senate passed the bill with only three "noes"; ten days later the House of Representatives rushed it through in four minutes by a vote of 84 to 4. Violators of the law were subject to a $500 fine or one year in jail.

As for legal action against the Klan by representatives of government on the local level, twenty-two southern cities had by the beginning of 1950 outlawed the wearing of masks in public. In Atlanta, Georgia, for example, the City Council in May, 1949, by a unanimous vote of 17 to 0 approved an ordinance to make masking one's face in public, except for festive occasions such as Halloween, an offense punishable by a fine of $200 and thirty days in jail.

From 1915 to 1944 all Knights owed fealty to one particular member of their order—the Imperial Wizard. It is true that in 1944 the Invisible Empire, Knights of the Ku Klux Klan was dissolved because of financial reasons, and the Association of Georgia Klans was formed. But as Grand Dragon of the latter organization, Samuel J. Green was the one individual in Klandom to whom all Knights paid homage. Just as soon as it was expedient, in August, 1949, at a Klonvokation held in Atlanta, Green assumed the coveted title of Imperial Wizard. Barely two weeks later, while working in his garden, he succumbed to a heart attack.

Immediately there appeared many pretenders to the throne of Klandom, each seeking the kind of allegiance historically due him as leader. The scramble for the post Green left vacant resulted in extensive injury to Klanism. The secret order splintered into many rival groups, each considering itself—or at least advertising as—the direct spiritual heir of the Invisible Empire, Knights of the Ku Klux Klan founded in 1915. Before 1949 came to an end, the number of Klans in operation approached the dozen mark.

The Association of Georgia Klans was not destroyed by the internecine competition; it survived, in fact, as the largest of the individual Klan organizations. Succeeding Green as Imperial Wizard of the Association of Georgia Klans on August 27, 1949, was Samuel W. Roper, a fifty-four year old former member of the Atlanta police force, who had taken a leave of absence in 1941-1942 to serve as Director of the Georgia Bureau of Investigation under Governor Eugene Talmadge. Roper had joined the Klan in 1921, but then disaffiliated himself until the Association of Georgia Klans was formed under Green's leadership in 1944.

Roper was bequeathed an organization containing an estimated 100,-000 members. Two months after taking office, Roper said he had Kleagles operating in ten states, and correspondence from thirty-two other states, where former Knights had founded individual Klans and were seeking affiliation with some higher body. Upon acceding to the Imperial Wizardship, Roper announced that he would continue the basic policies which his predecessor had ultimately come to follow; that is, an avowal of the spirit of charity toward Negroes, Catholics, and Jews,[3] plus a disavowal of the practice of physically disciplining wrongdoers. As to the local Klan's reforming of personal conduct in the community in which it existed, Roper declared that the chapter's course of action should consist of reporting the delinquent and his sins to the police, while at the same time giving to these law authorities its full moral support.

Impeding to some extent Roper's program of expansion during its first few months was the newly organized Federated Ku Klux Klans, Inc. Operating in the state of Alabama, its head was Imperial Wizard William Hugh Morris, a young roofing contractor from Birmingham. For refusing to turn over membership records to a grand jury investigating an outbreak of floggings in the Birmingham area, Morris spent sixty-seven days in jail in the summer of 1949. While incarcerated, he claimed there were 20,000 members in his order, and predicted that there would be 100,000 within a year, as a manifestation of the widespread arousement among Alabamans over his martyrdom.

A threat to the hegemony of Roper's order in Georgia and Morris' in Alabama was the Knights of the Ku Klux Klan of America. On August 23, 1949, in Montgomery, Alabama, about fifty representatives of splintered Klan groups in the states of Tennessee, Alabama, Mississippi, Louisiana, Arkansas, and Missouri formed this organization, claiming it to be of nationwide proportions. Consolidating into the Knights of the Ku Klux Klan of America were the following outfits: Independent Klans, Seashore Klans, Ozark Klans, Star Klans, River Valley Klans, and Allied Klans. All other Klan groups were asked to join this pseudo-national order. Both Roper's Association of Georgia Klans and Morris' Federated Ku Klux Klans, Inc. rejected the invitation.

Leading the Knights of the Ku Klux Klan of America as Imperial Emperor was a colorful individual with a name to match—Dr. Lycurgus Spinks.[4] Wearing his white hair down to his shoulders, covering himself with a multitude of fraternal pins, addressing every male except the most aged as "son," the sixty-five year old Spinks was the leader of an individual Klan in Thomasville, Alabama, ninety miles southwest of Montgomery. As a young man Spinks had become a Baptist clergyman, filling posts for a decade in the Carolinas and Arkansas. He was later expelled from the ministry. For a couple of years he earned a reputation as a sexologist, delivering "For Men Only" and "For Women Only" lectures. It was during this period of his career that he acquired the title "doctor."

Imperial Emperor Spinks claimed that the Knights of the Ku Klux Klan of America started with a membership of 265,000. This figure was viewed by Spinks' competitors as well as by contemporary journalists as an utterly gross exaggeration. The group based its ideals directly upon the native-born, white, Protestant philosophy of the Klan of the 1920's. It did go on record as opposed to the wearing of the hood in public.

In addition to the Roper, Morris, and Spinks Klans was a multiplication of rather shakily constituted orders. Characteristic of each of these were a leadership lacking in administrative skill, a membership never in excess of a few thousand, and—consequently—a life span that was short. The first of these small outfits to be formed was the Original Southern Klans, Inc., the Invisible Empire. It was established by two chapters bolted from the Association of Georgia Klans, the ones in Columbus and nearby Manchester. The head of this organization was Grand Wizard Alton Pate, a twenty-three year old World War II veteran and Kligrapp of the Columbus chapter of the Association of Georgia Klans before the rift had occurred. According to Pate, the aims of this order were the following: defense of Protestant Americanism, opposition to the "blending" of the white race with another, prevention of political dominance by "any inferior minority group," and resistance to the "teachings of the Communist party which embody advocacy of sexual equality under the guise of social equality." Ritualistically, the order banned the wearing of the hood except at formal ceremonies on its own property.

Farther north was the Association of Carolina Klans, headed by Grand Dragon Thomas L. Hamilton, a middle-aged wholesale grocer from Leesville, South Carolina, twenty-five miles west of Columbia. This group stood for "truth, right, and justice"—and, more specifically, white supremacy. Terrorism was disavowed. To his followers Grand Dragon Hamilton charged, "If you see something you don't like, don't mob up. Tell it to your law-enforcement officers. That's the way the Klan wants it." Unfortunately, members of the Association of Carolina Klans, including the Grand Dragon himself, soon dismissed from their minds the exhortation against "night-riding." On October 1, 1952, Hamilton began a four-year prison term for having masterminded an extensive program of terrorism. Fifteen of his followers received sentences averaging three years each and forty-nine others were fined a total of $18,250.

Giving Imperial Wizard Morris a bit of trouble in Alabama for a few months was a seventy-two year old physician from Birmingham named E. P. Pruitt. The septuagenarian organized the Federated Klans of Alabama, after having resigned from the Federated Ku Klux Klans, Inc. in July, 1949, over a row with Morris regarding the wear-

ing of the hood and the engaging in "night-riding." Pruitt was actively opposed to both practices. Neither was to have a place in his new
Federated Klans of Alabama. The physician even went so far as to
express the aim of discarding the robe. Pruitt's order was quite short-
lived.

In a geographic area including southern Georgia, northern Florida,
and eastern Alabama another Klan was functioning by the fall of 1949.
Calling itself the Original Southern Klans, Inc., it was formed by a
Columbus, Georgia, lawyer named Fred New and a radio preacher
named Jack Johnson. The New-Johnson outfit was held in little repute
by all the other Klans because it had altered much of the ritual and
discarded a great deal of the phraseology of Klanism as worked out by
Imperial Wizard Simmons three decades before.

Confined to the state of Florida was the Southern Knights of the
Ku Klux Klan. Its leader was Grand Dragon Bill Hendrix, a building
contractor from Tallahassee. If the beliefs of this outfit can be approached through a speech delivered by its Grand Dragon in the fall
of 1951, then the Southern Knights of the Ku Klux Klan bitterly opposed
Negroes; Jews; Communists; the Congress of Industrial Organizations;
and anything that smacked of liberalism, including people such as
Eleanor Roosevelt, places such as the University of North Carolina,
and things such as the *Louisville Courier-Journal*.

Also operating in Florida was the United Klan. This group was led
by C. L. Parker, a furniture dealer from River Junction, close to the
Georgia border. One hundred thousand members made up his order,
Parker claimed. If the New-Johnson body was held in low esteem by
members of other Klans for tampering too much with the ornamental
aspect of Klanism, then the Parker order was indescribably loathed, for
it desecrated the ideology. In October, 1953, Parker announced that
the United Klan would open its membership to Negroes! This was
to be done, he quickly explained, as a pleasant learning experience in
the worthwhileness of segregation. Thus, the Negro Knights would
be ruled by Negro Cyclopses in Negro Klaverns. To join the United
Klan a Negro had to pay $1 in cash and take an oath of allegiance to
God and the Constitution. There is no indication that the United Klan
was besieged with requests for application forms from the colored
population.

At the end of 1949 there was reason for believing that there would
be cohesion in Klanism once more. On November 22, it was announced that as a direct result of a conference between Imperial
Wizard Roper of the Association of Georgia Klans and Imperial Wizard

Morris of the Federated Ku Klux Klans, Inc., these two orders had reached a "working agreement" which would eventually lead to consolidation. Such a fusion would have united the two largest Klans in the South, leaving the small splinter groups to wend their respective ways to probable extinction. But nothing more of the "working agreement" was heard from either Roper or Morris. Perhaps the latter began to have misgivings about such an undertaking, fearing that it would quickly turn into an absorption of his group by Roper's much larger one. Whatever the reason, consolidation of the Association of Georgia Klans and the Federated Ku Klux Klans, Inc. never took place.

Consequently, Morris turned elsewhere in search for unity. On December 18, he, Grand Dragon Hendrix of the Southern Knights of the Ku Klux Klan and Grand Dragon Hamilton of the Association of Carolina Klans announced that collectively they would act as the "governing body" of Klanism. In this case the Federated Ku Klux Klans, Inc., would clearly be dominant. But this proposed consolidation also never materialized.

During the early 1950's there were indications that the Klan might disappear permanently from the American scene. As any search through newspapers and magazines of the period will show, practically the only activities in which the Klan engaged pertained to its role of self-appointed protector of a community's morals and peace. Ostracism, boycotting, the sending of threatening letters, "night-riding" — at such measures the press scolded, the public was enraged. The Klan could never remain in existence solely as a maltreater of erring citizens.

Quite suddenly, however, in 1954, the order took a new lease on life. For the next few years rapid growth was the keynote of Klanism. In the South thousands of fiery crosses lighted up the night. By 1958 there were well over 100,000 new Knights and more than 500 new chapters in the various Klans. The reason? On May 17, 1954, the Supreme Court outlawed the segregation of races in the public schools. The following year, on May 31, 1955, this tribunal instructed the lower federal courts to see that the schools made "a prompt and reasonable start" toward desegregation and proceeded "with all deliberate speed." In the mid-1930's the Klan had intentionally sought a new issue (it soon latched on to anti-Communism) upon which to regain its former strength — and failed. In the mid-1950's the Klan had thrust upon it a new issue — and thereby was able to resuscitate temporarily.

In manifesting its opposition to desegregation the Klan used various methods and techniques. There was an outburst of activity in Alabama.

In September, 1956, more than 1,000 inhabitants of Montgomery went to a baseball grounds parking lot to listen to Klan orators advise them how to resist desegregation of any kind. Two months later scores of Knights gathered together with hundreds of Klan sympathizers at an auto race track just outside of the city to hear the Supreme Court vigorously denounced. This rally, by the way, was preceded by a sidewalk stroll through downtown Montgomery by robed Klansmen. At the very end of 1956 and the beginning of 1957 there was an outbreak of terrorism in the city. Bombed were Negro churches as well as homes of Negro ministers who insistently expressed their advocacy of integration of the races in the use of public facilities. On February 10, 1957, Chief of Police G. J. Ruppenthal announced that investigation showed that each bombing was perpetrated by members of the Klan.

In Birmingham, in August, 1956, 200 Knights, under the blaze of three fiery crosses, held a rally to voice their collective resistance to the Supreme Court ruling. The following January a Klan leader told 250 robed figures assembled in the city (not only were the Knights in costume, but also their spouses and offspring) that the fraternity would "not give another inch or another concession" in its opposition to desegregation.

About 100 shouting, horn-blowing robed members of the Klan in Mobile drove up to the home of Mrs. Dorothy D. Daponte in September, 1956, and set fire to a cross ten feet high as a protest against her attempts to have a foster daughter, the child of a former Negro domestic, admitted to a public school previously attended only by whites.

In Florida, less than two weeks after the May, 1954, Supreme Court decision, Grand Dragon Bill Hendrix of the Southern Knights of the Ku Klux Klan resigned from his fraternal post and announced his candidacy for the governorship on a pro-segregation platform. If elected, "there will be no Negroes going to white schools or whites going to Negro schools," he promised. His plan was to ask for write-in votes in November. Hendrix's successor as Grand Dragon of the Southern Knights of the Ku Klux Klan instructed his underlings to distribute petitions against desegregation in the schools of the Sunshine State. The petitions were addressed to Acting Governor Charley Johnson, the State Board of Education, and county school boards.

Also in Florida, in July, 1956, 200 hooded and robed members of the Klan and 1,000 sympathizers in street clothes gathered outside of Lakeland, twenty-five miles northeast of Tampa, to protest any move whatever toward school desegregation. During the course of the rally hillbilly music was played, a cross was set ablaze, perfervid speeches were delivered by three Knights, and 3,000 application forms were distributed to the non-Klan spectators. The following month, in an open field just south of Starke, while 500 spectators witnessed the event from behind a roped off area, 125 hooded and robed Knights cheered one of their leaders lustily as he denounced the Supreme Court.

On September 29, 1956, in a pasture not far from Atlanta, Georgia, the Klan held its biggest rally since the advent of World War II. More than 3,500 Knights from at least five southern states, accompanied by their wives and children, heard leaders emphasize that their order would stay within "laws that are just" in its battle against desegregation.

The football field of a public high school attended only by whites in Summerville, Georgia, which lies in the extreme northwestern part of the state, was ordered padlocked in November, 1956, against use by two teams from all-Negro schools following a protest by a purported Klan leader of the area. The game had been arranged by the local Junior Chamber of Commerce to raise funds for the white high school band.

In July, 1956, a Methodist church school in Camden, South Carolina, thirty miles northeast of Columbia, was forced to close down because of possible violence against the integrated group of fifteen students in attendance. There had been a rash of anonymous telephone calls to the church authorities threatening to blow up the building or burn it down. In addition, a cross had been burned in front of the school. The mayor of the town, Henry Savage, publicly blamed the entire incident on a revival of Klanism since the Supreme Court ruling. Camden was not to see the end of agitation over the segregation issue. Less than a half year later Guy Hutchins, the band director of the local all-white high school, was flogged by a group of men for allegedly preaching integration in public institutions of learning. Of the six men arrested for the act of terrorism, at least one admitted being a member of the Klan.

Two mass meetings were held on July 28, 1956, in South Carolina, one at Columbia and the other at Hartsville, sixty miles away. Hooded and robed Knights denounced the Supreme Court and desegregation. At the Hartsville rally a Klan orator who identified himself to members of the press only as a "country preacher from down the road" called President Dwight D. Eisenhower a "low-down scoundrel" for having carried out after World War II, as Chief of Staff of the United States Army, integration in his branch of the service.

In March, 1958, three members of the Klan in North Carolina were sentenced to prison for terms varying from two to ten years. The action taken against them was the end result of the manner in which these Knights protested against desegregation in the Tar Heel State — attempting to bomb, on February, 1957, a Negro elementary school outside of Charlotte.

The Klan was not the only organization to resist desegregation in the public schools of the South. Two months after the May 17, 1954, Supreme Court decision, there was formed in Indianola, Mississippi, a hamlet which lies close to the Arkansas border, the White Citizens Council. Within a year branches of the new outfit sprang up all over Dixie. By 1957 the White Citizens Council had some 300,000 members in more than 500 chapters. Its strongest backing came from the Deep South, where the ratio of Negroes to whites has always been high. The state of Mississippi alone, for example, contained more than one-fourth of the membership of the Council.

It would be well to contrast the Council with the Klan. First, from the very beginning the Council carried out its program in the open. Public auditoriums and theaters were used for meetings. Members made no attempt to shield from others their affiliation with the group. Second, in striving to create an image of "respectability," it studiously avoided extremism. There was to be no donning of regalia, engaging in ritual, or participating in terrorism. Third, as a result of the preceding policies it enlisted the support of the most esteemed citizens. Among those who joined the Council were, for example, the following: in Louisiana a state senator, a state university board supervisor, and a former president of the state medical association; in Alabama three state senators and the mayor of Montgomery; in North Carolina several leading industrialists, three former Speakers of the state Assembly, a state university medical school professor, and a former United States Attorney.

Did these basic differences between the Council and the Klan preclude all intercourse? The answer is "no." Much of the anti-integration literature distributed by the two organizations was identical. Also, in many localities individuals belonged to both groups at the same time. The secretary-treasurer of the Association of White Citizens Councils of Florida, Homer Barrs, said in an interview, "We don't bar Klan members from joining the Councils. Any white person who does not belong to the NAACP is eligible." Then, too, Council leaders addressed Klan meetings. Doing more of this than anyone else was John Kasper, secretary of the White Citizens Council of Washington, D. C. He appeared before groups of Knights — in Alabama in the fall of 1956, in Florida in the spring of 1957, in Tennessee in the summer of 1957 — to urge the Klan to co-operate with the Council in preaching the "segregation gospel."[6]

While the battle against desegregation in the public schools of the South was taking place, the multiplication of Klans was going on. There seemed to be a spewing forth! By 1958 there were so many different splinter groups that the tabulation of them is unreliable. The factionalism that resulted was more than a lack of centralized authority in Klanism; it was internecine warfare.

The dominant organization was the U. S. Klans, Knights of the Ku Klux Klan. Its head was Imperial Wizard Eldon Lee Edwards, a forty-eight year old paint sprayer at an automobile body plant in Atlanta. Edwards' order was the direct descendant of the Association of Georgia Klans that had been led by Imperial Wizards Green and Roper. In 1950 Edwards assumed leadership of the Association of Georgia Klans, reorganized it slightly, and renamed it the U. S. Klans, Knights of the Ku Klux Klan.

Outside the home state of Georgia, Edwards' order was most active in South Carolina, Alabama, and Louisiana. As a matter of fact, the Grand Dragon of the U. S. Klans, Knights of the Ku Klux Klan in each of these states wielded more power and earned a greater reputation than the actual heads of the other Klan groups in existence. The Grand Dragon of the Realm of South Carolina was James H. Bickley, a carpenter from Marion, close to the North Carolina border. Within three months after taking office, he increased the number of chapters in the Palmetto State from twenty to thirty-five. "I ain't got nothing against niggers," Bickley remarked on one occasion. "I don't believe most of them would be causing any trouble if it wasn't for the NAACP and the Jews. I understand there are a lot of Communists . . . trying to get us to integrate with the niggers so we'll breed down the race."

The Grand Dragon of the Realm of Alabama was Alvin Horn, an electrical worker and self-proclaimed Baptist minister from Talladega, fifty miles east of Birmingham. When he assumed his duties as Grand Dragon in the summer of 1956, there were but two chapters of the U. S. Klans, Knights of the Ku Klux Klan in Alabama. Less than a year later there were more than 100.

A Baton Rouge welder named Edgar Taylor was the Grand Dragon of the Realm of Louisiana. "The niggers are the main thing with us now," Taylor told a journalist in the spring of 1957. "We are not fighting Jews and Catholics except where they help the niggers."

On a nationwide television program in 1957 Imperial Wizard Edwards maintained that "God Almighty created the races and segregated them, sent them each on their own destiny." As for his Klan's program of opposition to desegregation in the schools, violence in any form would be shunned.

Edwards refused to divulge the numerical strength of his Klan, giving as a reason the fact that it was a secret fraternity. The membership was estimated by contemporary observers to be about 50,000. Whatever the size of the U. S. Klans, Knights of the Ku Klux Klan, it was the largest of all the orders. Edwards asserted that it was the "one true Klan." The other organizations were "outlaws and counterfeiters." But verbalization on the part of the Imperial Wizard — however emphatic it may have been — could not check the luxuriance of Klans.

The largest order next to the U. S. Klans, Knights of the Ku Klux Klan was the Florida Ku Klux Klan, with a membership of about 30,000. Somewhere at the top of the hierarchy of this organization was J. E. Fraser, a nurseryman from Macclenny, twenty-five miles west of Jacksonville. Reputed to be the leader of the Florida Ku Klux Klan as Grand Wizard, Fraser consistently denied holding that office, but at the same time maintained that he could always speak for the individual who did. According to Fraser, the Florida Ku Klux Klan stood for white supremacy, segregation, and "upholding the law." "There's plenty of ways to do things within the law and sometimes we have to straighten up the officials," he said. "Fellow sells his house to a nigger in a white neighborhood and we just spread the word. He loses his business and his friends. That . . . boy better just get out of this state."

Probably next in size was the Association of South Carolina Klans.' The name of the head of this group was kept from the public. Acting as spokesman for it was the Kligrapp of the chapter in Columbia, Robert E. Hodges. A student at a business college in that city, the twenty-four year old Hodges declared that the activities of the Association of South Carolina Klans were directed primarily against Negroes, but also against Catholics and Jews whenever the latter two made efforts to help Negroes achieve civil rights or social equality.

Operating at opposite ends of Alabama were two small but extremely aggressive organizations. In the northern part of the state was the Original Ku Klux Klan of the Confederacy, led by Asa Carter, a young radio announcer from Birmingham who had been expelled from the White Citizens Council for his extremist activities. Perhaps the most violent of all the orders, the Original Ku Klux Klan of the Confederacy conducted blood-rite initiation ceremonies, sanctioned the carrying of weapons by its members, and directed extraordinarily abusive harangues against Negroes, Catholics, and Jews.

In the southern part of Alabama the Gulf Ku Klux Klan carried on. Heading it as Imperial Wizard was a gunsmith from Mobile named Elmo C. Barnard. According to him, the Gulf Ku Klux Klan stood for free speech, a free press, free public schools, white supremacy, "just" laws, "the pursuit of happiness," and American rejection of foreign creeds. Barnard condemned terrorism as basic policy for any group, but said a "little violence" might have to be resorted to in resolving the conflict between Negroes and whites.

Across the Mississippi River in Louisiana was an ineffectual group called the Knights of the Ku Klux Klan, led by the Rev. Perry E. Strickland, the founder of the Central Baptist Mission just outside of Baton Rouge. Strickland stated that some Catholics who were opposed to desegregation of the races in the public schools attempted to join his order, but were unhesitatingly turned down. "We need a white Protestant group based on American principles," the minister concluded.

A triology of Klans functioned in Arkansas. In addition to two small groups, the Association of Arkansas Klans and the Original Ku Klux Klan, was Edwards' order, with A. C. Hightower, a barber by trade, acting as Grand Dragon. According to Hightower, his followers were "strictly law-abiding citizens."[8]

Just as Klanism was vivified in 1954 by the occurrence of an outside event, the Supreme Court decision on segregation, so to a lesser extent was it in 1960. For on July 13 of that year, in Los Angeles, California, the national convention of the Democratic party chose as its nominee for the presidency a Catholic, Senator John F. Kennedy of Massachusetts. Fiery crosses were soon in evidence throughout Dixie. There were at night Klan parades and rallies. Before long, in some cities of the Deep South Knights even dared to walk the streets in broad daylight wearing their hoods and robes. What effect did the activity of the Klan have upon the outcome of the ensuing election? To give as complete an answer as possible, it would be well to compare the presidential campaign of 1960 with the one of 1928, in which the Democratic standard-bearer also was a Catholic, Governor Alfred E. Smith of New York.

It is not difficult to find the reasons for the defeat of the Democratic candidate in 1928. In addition to the existence of a belief on the part of many that the general prosperity of the times would soon disappear without Republican rule, there was widespread opposition to Smith because of his anti-prohibitionism, his Tammany connections, his "alienism," and his Catholicism.

Nineteen sixty was different. Kennedy was not a "wet" who had incurred the wrath of the Anti-Saloon League and Woman's Christian Temperance Union. He was not associated with a local party organization known for its flagrant political abuses. He did not represent the "alienism" of a metropolis; neither did he even give an appearance of so doing, for he was rich, well-educated, handsomely fair, tastefully groomed, cultivated in speech. Kennedy was, however, a Catholic. The standard-bearer of the Democratic party in 1928 failed to win the election not because of his Catholicism. Still, his religious affiliation was unquestionably a factor in the defeat. In 1960 many a non-Catholic voter was ready to cast a ballot for a Catholic presidential nominee whose party, record, and campaign promises were to his liking. The West Virginia Democratic presidential primary of May 10, 1960, offers a superb illustration of this. Facing the voters were Kennedy and the Protestant Senator Hubert Humphrey of Minnesota, each comparable to the other in youth, personableness, and legislative voting record. The pollsters anticipated Kennedy's defeat on the religious issue. When the final returns were in, he had won handily, receiving 235,738 votes to Humphrey's 149,214. The surprising victory took place for many reasons. Compared with the Humphreyites, the Kennedy forces spent a considerably greater amount of money; were much more efficiently organized; and had Franklin D. Roosevelt, Jr., stump the state to convince the miners, the vast majority of whom looked back on the New Deal with nostalgia, that the Senator from Massachusetts was the spiritual descendant of F. D. R. Most political observers considered Kennedy himself to be the biggest factor in the landslide. One popular news magazine had this to say: "His easy manner, serious speeches and kinetic charm, his decision to fight out the religious issue, and even his Harvard accent—all won respect and votes."

It is difficult to assess the effect of Klan activity upon the outcome of the election of 1928, for there were other influential groups as well as prominent religious figures and bolting Democratic leaders attacking Smith for one or more of the same reasons as were given by the secret fraternity for its opposition to the Democratic candidate.

Ninteen sixty was similar. Along with the Klan were organizations and individuals hostile to Kennedy for the very same reasons; namely, his Catholicism and his stand on civil rights. The Democratic national convention adopted for 1960 a civil rights plank that reached far beyond anything on this issue included in any previous platform of either major political party. According to the plank, the Democratic party endorsed the "equal access for all Americans to all areas of community life, including voting booths, schoolrooms, jobs, housing and public facilities"; advocated that the Attorney-General be "directed to file civil injunction suits in federal courts to prevent the denial of any civil rights on grounds of race, creed or color"; and proposed the establishment of a federal Fair Employment Practices Commission to "secure for everyone the right to equal opportunity for employment." In accepting the nomination of his party, Kennedy declared, "This is a platform on which I can run with enthusiasm and with conviction." Taking an active part in the effort to swing certain of the customarily Democratic states to the standard-bearer of the Republican party, Vice-President Richard M. Nixon, were, for example, such organizations as the White Citizens Council; the Church of Christ, a Fundamentalist denomination centered in Tennessee; and the Citizens for Religious Freedom,° and such individuals as Dr. Baines M. Cook, the chief administrator of the activities of the Disciples of Christ; and Dr. Ramsey Pollard, President of the Southern Baptist Convention.

As for southern Democratic leaders, not one came out publicly against the titular head of his party because he was Catholic, as Senator J. Thomas Heflin of Alabama had done thirty-two years before. But the Democratic politicians of Dixie were unhappy—extremely unhappy—with Kennedy's position on civil rights. Nixon was enthusiastically welcomed in Georgia by Mayor William B. Hartsfield of Atlanta and quite popular former gubernatorial candidate James V. Carmichael, the latter going so far as to pledge publicly his support of the Republican presidential nominee. Senator Harry F. Byrd of Virginia failed to give the nod to Kennedy. Senator J. Strom Thurmond of South Carolina declared that he could abide neither the party's "obnoxious and punitive" platform nor its standard-bearer. James F. Byrnes, who during the course of his career served as Associate Justice of the Supreme Court, Secretary of State under Truman, and Governor of his home state of South Carolina, condemned the civil rights plank of the party's platform and announced himself for the Republican ticket. After sitting on their hands for almost three months after the Democratic convention was held, Senators Herman Talmadge and Richard B. Russell of Georgia raised them gingerly in favor of their colleague from Massachusetts. Meeting on

September 20, in Dallas, the Texas Democratic convention adopted a plank in its state platform that was diametrically opposed to the civil rights plank in the party's national platform. Not until the end of September, at the twenty-sixth annual Southern Governors Conference, did ten of the chief executives of states south of the Mason-Dixon line abandon their lukewarm stand during the campaign to give full support to Kennedy.

It is most difficult to prove that playing a determining role in the presidential election of 1928 was an order that had recently been censured by the American public for its excesses, lost its political potency, and suffered a sharp drop in membership. If the Klan was indeed a factor in the desertion of almost half the "Solid South" to the Republican candidate, Herbert Hoover, then it was not the substance but the spirit of the fraternity that made it so.

Nineteen sixty? There are scattered examples of the Klan's engaging in political activity of national significance. In 1958 Imperial Wizard Edwards' order, the U.S. Klans, Knights of the Ku Klux Klan, worked in Alabama for the election of John Patterson to the highest office in the state. Patterson realized his gubernatorial aspirations. When, months before the Democratic national convention of 1960, he endorsed Kennedy as his personal choice for the presidency, he was visited by a thirty-two man delegation headed by the Kladd of the Klan in Prattville, just outside of Montgomery. The Alabama chief executive was asked if it had ever occurred to him that he was "being used as a guinea pig by the Communist-Jewish integrators" to sample the political sentiment of the South for the Senator from Massachusetts. And just before the conclusion of the presidential campaign, representatives of various chapters of the U.S. Klans, Knights of the Ku Klux Klan in the Gulf state attended a meeting held in the Tuscaloosa County courthouse, at which the newly appointed Grand Dragon of the Realm of Alabama, Bob Shelton, exhorted, "Klansmen should stay away from Kennedy and keep an eye on John Patterson. ... They are the tools of the Jews."

Klan leaders in Florida spoke out. The Grand Dragon of the U.S. Klans, Knights of the Ku Klux Klan in that state, William J. Griffin, announced himself in September, 1960, for the nominee of the G. O. P.[10] Boosting Governor Orval E. Faubus of Arkansas for the presidency on the National States' Rights ticket was Bill Hendrix, who was once more head of the Southern Knights of the Ku Klux Klan as Grand Dragon, after having resigned from his fraternal post in 1954 to run for the governorship of Florida on a pro-segregation platform.

In a communication sent out to every member of the Association of South Carolina Klans, Robert E. Hodges, the Kligrapp of the chapter in Columbia, declared: "You cannot afford to support or vote for anyone or group that represents the Roman Catholic Church. To do so is to vote against your God, and Savior, and your church, your country and even yourself since the Catholic Church is directly opposed to Protestant churches, your America, and especially you as a Protestant. . Heaven help your soul if you vote away your religious liberty . . . "

In the Upper South, John Kasper of the White Citizens Council went before many Klan groups to attack Kennedy's candidacy. If the Senator from Massachusetts happened to be successful in his bid for the presidency, Kasper iterated, he should be "impeached before the sun rises."

The presidential election of 1960 turned out to be the closest in modern times. Kennedy won the electoral vote of the southern half of New England, the Middle Atlantic states, plus most of the "Solid South"; Nixon carried four states of Dixie—Virginia, Kentucky, Tennessee, and Florida,[11] nearly all of the north central and mountain states, plus the entire Pacific coast. In popular votes, Kennedy received 34,221,355 to Nixon's 34,109,398. This was a plurality for the Democrat of 111,957 over his opponent, representing less than two-tenths of 1 per cent of the total number of votes cast—the smallest percentage difference between the popular votes of two presidential candidates since the election of 1884.

The effectiveness of the political proceedings by the secret order during the campaign is problematical. The Klan declined in power as Election Day, November 8, 1960, approached. There are two basic reasons for this, in addition to widespread public repulsion at the terrorism of the order. First, the White Citizens Council, in its shunning all extremist measures, lured away from the Klan the vast majority of Southerners desiring to join an organization that would battle for the status quo in racial matters. Second, the Klan was literally being ripped apart by the continual formation of splinter groups. By 1960 the number of separate orders was not even definitely known; it was changing too frequently. A high-ranking Knight in Florida pointed out that there were so many different Klan groups in existence that the old passwords and counter-signs were unusable. One southern newspaper tittered that so many Klans were operating in Dixie that it was "impossible to tell the Grand Dragons, Wizards, and Kleagles apart without a program."

Thus, if the Klan was a factor in the desertion of a portion of the

"Solid South" to the Republican nominee in the presidential election of 1960, then it was the spirit and not the substance of the secret order that made it so—as had been the case in the presidential election of 1928.

REFERENCES

Chapter I

1. *The Ku Klux Klan,* 67 Cong., 1 Sess. (Washington, 1921), 121, contains this description of the elements as recollected by William Joseph Simmons. A stenographic record of the hearings on Klan activities held before the House Committee on Rules, October 11-17, 1921, this will be cited hereafter as *Klan Hearings.*

2. It appears that Simmons was at one point discharged for inefficiency as a salesman of men's garters.

3. *Klan Hearings,* 67-68.

4. In *Klan Hearings,* 67, appears the following statement by Simmons: "They call me 'Colonel,' largely out of respect. Every lawyer in Georgia is called 'Colonel,' so they thought that I was as good as a lawyer, so they call me that. . . . I was at one time the senior colonel in command of five regiments and colonel of my own regiment of the uniform rank of the Woodmen of the World, and I was known as 'Colonel.' I have used that title on certain literature of the klan for the reason that there are three other 'W. J. Simmonses' in Atlanta, and for some time our mail got confused. It is merely a designation. They accord it to me as an honor and I appreciate it."

5. *Klansman's Manual, Compiled and Issued Under Direction and Authority of the Knights of the Ku Klux Klan, Incorporated* (n.p., 1924), chap. III, sec. II. For detailed information on the operation of the local Klan chapter, see the pamphlet, *Klan Building. An Outline of Proven Klan Methods for Successfully Applying the Art of Klankraft in Building and Operating Local Klans* (Atlanta, 1923).

6. See *Kloran, Knights of the Ku Klux Klan: First Degree Character* (Atlanta, 1916), which was undoubtedly written by Simmons. The pamphlet, *Delivery of Chapter. Issued by Imperial Palace, Invisible Empire, Knights of the Ku Klux Klan* (Atlanta, 1923), also sets forth the order of the Klonklave.

7. These were all duly copyrighted in Simmons's name. Years later he received from the Klan a great sum of money for these copyrights.

8. "Many wise men," Simmons once stated, "have puzzled over that motto. They said it wasn't Latin and it wasn't Greek. I made the motto up myself. It's part Latin and part Saxon. 'Non' and 'sed,' of course, are Latin. But I was reliably informed that 'Silba' is an old Saxon word meaning 'self' and 'anthar' means 'others.' So, you see, 'Not for self, but for others.' Simple enough." In William G. Shepherd, "How I Put Over the Klan," *Collier's,* July 14, 1928, p. 32.

9. Winfield Jones, *The True Story of the Ku Klux Klan* (n.p., 1921), 52, states that Simmons did get appreciable assistance from three men: Imperial Kligrapp Louis D. Wade, a cotton mill superintendent; Imperial Klabee H. C. Montgomery, an Atlanta optician; and "Imperial Klonsel," or legal advisor, Paul S. Etheridge, a lawyer and member of the Fulton County Board of Commissioners of Roads and Revenues.

10. *Klan Hearings,* 69.

11. For the text of the contract, see *Klan Hearings,* 32.

12. Quoted in "For and Against the Ku Klux Klan," *The Literary Digest,* September 24, 1921, p. 38.

13. For a list of all the Kleagles active at this time, see *New York World,* September 9, 1921, p. 2.

14. Atlanta remained the lead city of Klan activity until 1928, when the organization established a new national headquarters in Washington, D. C.

15. Testimony of Simmons in Case 1897 in Equity (1927), U. S. District Court, Pittsburgh.

16. Stanley Frost, "When the Klan Rules," *The Outlook,* December 26, 1923, p. 717. Frost's study of the Klan appears in eleven consecutive issues of *The Outlook.*

17. In Edward Price Bell, *Creed of the Klansman* (Chicago, 1924), 8, appears a defense Evans once made of the wearing of the hood: it "protects scores of thousands of our members from intimidation, sabotage, and worse, and it screens our leaders from the temptation to forget the general interest in the pursuit of particular whims or ambitions. Self-esteem is eliminated. There is no lure of personal vanity nor of demagogy."

18. See *The Whole Truth About the Effort to Destroy the Klan* (Atlanta, 1923), which is a pamphlet Evans ordered published to show how self-seeking men had gathered about Simmons in order to rule the Klan for personal gain.

19. Marion Monteval [pseud. of Edgar Irving Fuller?], *The Klan Inside Out* (Claremore, Okla., [c. 1924]), 51; C. Anderson Wright, *The Ku Klux Klan, As Exposed by Major C. Anderson Wright ... and as Defended by Col. Wm. J. Simmons* (Atlanta, 1923), 16.

20. In July, 1922, Imperial Kligrapp Louis D. Wade filed suit alleging that Clarke had gained complete control over Simmons by taking advantage of his continual drunken condition.

21. W. M. Likins, *Patriotism Capitalized: or, Religion Turned into Gold* (Uniontown, Pa., 1925), 126.

22. For the case against Stephenson, see Edgar Allen Booth, *The Mad Mullah of America* (Columbus, 1927); for the case for him, see Robert A. Butler. *"So They Framed Stephenson"* (Huntington, Ind., 1940). (In 1956 Stephenson was released from prison.)

23. Of the 115,000,000 Americans in the 1920's, 20,000,000 were foreign born; 10,000,000, Negro; 20,000,000, Catholic; and almost 3,000,000, Jewish.

24. Since the Klan, as a secret fraternity, never published its numerical strength, each figure given in this paragraph is an approximation based upon recollections of Klan leaders or estimates by contemporary reporters and later students of the organization.

CHAPTER II

1. In the *Washington, D. C. Fellowship Forum,* November 24, 1923, p. 2, there appear for comparison two maps of the nation showing the expansion of the Klan, one reproduced from the *New York Herald* of November 11, 1923, and the other from the *New York Times* of November 12, 1923. Although the two maps do not agree in particulars, both show quite vividly that the Klan was powerful in the

Deep South, in the territory west of the lower Mississippi River, on the Pacific coast, and in the Middle West.

2. In the vigorously pro-Klan pamphlet, George E. Hills, *The Ku Klux Klan of the Present Day* (1923), 3, is found the following peculiar denial of the secret order's limiting its membership solely to Protestants: "Any Jew can belong if he believes in the divinity of Christ, any Catholic if he can fulfill the obligations of membership." Although the Klan at all times excluded women from membership, wives of Klansmen did form groups auxiliary to the local chapters. In the summer of 1927 the "Women of the Ku Klux Klan" went so far as to hold a national convention and adopt a constitution, which was never recognized by Klan national headquarters.

3. The number of Protestant ministers who condemned the Klan is, of course, legion. Such clergymen were horrified that a secret order which fostered racial and religious prejudice should attempt to speak in the name of the Protestant church.

4. Leaders of the revived Klan were fairly quick to realize the value of Griffith's masterpiece in their propaganda activities. For example, the *Jackson, Mississippi Daily Clarion-Ledger*, August 10, 1924, p. 16, contains a three-quarters page high endorsement of "The Birth of a Nation" by the Jackson Klan No. 22, Realm of Mississippi, in which the Exalted Cyclops wrote the following: "I feel sure that all good Americans in our city and surrounding territory, both men and women [,] will come to see this wonderful picture."

5. John Moffatt Mecklin, *The Ku Klux Klan, A Study of the American Mind* (New York, 1924), 157, states that he found, through many personal interviews with, and a questionnaire to, representative citizens from all parts of the nation who had become Klansmen, that the selling-point which gained most members for the secret order was undoubtedly anti-Catholicism.

6. The practice of "night-riding" was more prevalent among the Klansmen of the South than among those of other sections of the nation. "The Rise and Fall of the K. K. K.," *The New Republic*, November 30, 1927, p. 33, declares, "Some hoodlums signed up in order to participate in the night riding; but it is safe to say that 90 percent of the total membership list never indulged in such practices."

7. *Catalogue of Official* [Ku Klux Klan] *Robes and Banners* (Atlanta, 1925). For carrying the costume, a "rubberoid" case with separate compartments for hood and robe could be had for $1. The Gate City Manufacturing Company of Atlanta, which after 1920 was under contract to make the official Klan regalia, realized a profit of about $4 on every $5 costume it produced. The costume was merely rented to a Klansman and was to be returned if the member resigned from the organization.

8. Occasionally witnesses of a Klan parade were hostile to the marchers to the extent of actually attacking them. See, for example, *The Martyred Klansman, In Which Events Leading Up to the Shooting to Death of Klansman Thomas Rankin Abbott, on August 25, 1923, are Related* . . . . (Pittsburgh, 1923). As for the only national parade held by the order — in Washington, D. C., on August 8, 1925 — most reporters estimated that there were from 50,000 to 60,000 in the three hour and forty minute march down Pennsylvania Avenue.

9. Of the secondary works on the Ku Klux Klan of the Reconstruction period, three of the best are Stanley Fitzgerald Horn, *Invisible Empire, The Story of the Ku Klux Klan, 1866-1871* (Boston, 1939); Susan Lawrence Davis, *Authentic*

History, Ku Klux Klan, 1860-1877 (New York, 1934); W. B. Romine and Mrs. W. B. Romine, *Story of the Original Ku Klux Klan* (Pulaski, Tenn., 1934).

10. *Ideals of the Ku Klux Klan* (Atlanta, 1923), 3-4.

11. It must not be overlooked that this championing of things Protestant and native-born makes the Klan of the 1920's appear to be the successor more to two nineteenth century nativist organizations, the Know-Nothing party and the American Protective Association, than to its namesake. One of the best general accounts of Know-Nothingism can be found in Louis Dow Scisco, *Political Nativism in New York* (New York, 1901). A standard work on the American Protective Association is Humphrey J. Desmond, *The A. P. A. Movement, A Sketch* (Washington, 1912). A good brief coverage of both movements is found in Gustavus Myers, *History of Bigotry in the United States* (New York, 1943), chaps. XVIII-XXII.

12. John Moffatt Mecklin, *The Ku Klux Klan, A Study of the American Mind* (New York, 1924), 100, states that Baptists were "apparently the religious mainstay of the Klan."

13. A hint of how the local Klan lent assistance to its own can be acquired from *Ku Klux Klan, Realm of Indiana, Marion County Klan No. 3. Local Constitution* (Marion, Ind., 1924), art. VI, sec. 2, which states that donations were not to exceed $4 a week for each member of a distressed Klan family, and relief was not to be extended for more than six weeks, except by the authorization of the Kludd.

14. Of all the cases of Klan terrorism during the 1920's the Mer Rouge murder incident is undoubtedly the most notorious. The amount of contemporary literature dealing with the facts and results of the episode is quite extensive.

CHAPTER III

1. Stanley Frost, "When the Klan Rules," *The Outlook,* February 20, 1924, p. 310, writes that in nearly 90 per cent of the election contests he had been able to check, the Klan apparently had cast a practically solid vote.

CHAPTER IV

1. It should perhaps be stated at this point why the participation of the southern wing of the Klan in the election of representatives to Congress is treated in this chapter. The reason is that although representatives are members of the national government, they are elected by the voters, and reflect the political thinking, of a specific local area within a particular state.

2. The Klan's attempt to hold a meeting in Louisville was abandoned, and the activities of the fraternity were finally transferred to Jeffersonville, Indiana, opposite Louisville on the Ohio River.

3. Supplied by J. B. Stoner in an interview with Stetson Kennedy, December 12, 1945. In Stetson Kennedy Papers, New York Public Library, Harlem Branch.

4. J. P. Alley's cartoons and C. P. J. Mooney's editorials against the extremely active local Klan in Memphis won a Pulitzer Prize for their newspaper, the *Memphis Commercial-Appeal,* in 1922.

5. The word "promptly" used in the text is taken from the account in the *Raleigh News and Observer,* November 7, 1924, p. 2. Owned and published by the well-known Democratic politician, Josephus Daniels, the anti-Klan *Raleigh News and Observer* was a highly reliable and respectable newspaper. Taking

all this into consideration, it requires just a bit of reading between the lines to detect the probable positive relationship between Mayor Williams and the local Klan in Ahoskie.

6. In Josephus Daniels Papers, Library of Congress.

7. *Klan Hearings*, 74.

8. In Stetson Kennedy Papers, New York Public Library, Harlem Branch.

9. The *New York Times*, September 21, 1922, p. 2, notes that Sims "if not a member of the Klan is closely affiliated with the organization."

10. In his reply to the attacks upon the local Klan by the Pulaski County Democratic convention Cook referred to Dodge as an "ex-Klansman lawyer, who has been suspended."

CHAPTER V

1. *Klan Hearings*, 26-27.

2. For a highly informative biographical sketch of Upshaw, see *Washington, D. C. Fellowship Forum*, April 11, 1925, p. 4. Upshaw was known for his interest and participation in the causes of prohibition, Fundamentalism, and Americanism. For his thoughts on these and other matters, see William D. Upshaw, *Clarion Calls From Capitol Hill* (New York, 1923).

3. *Klan Hearings*, 67.

4. *Klan Hearings*, 86-87.

5. C. Vann Woodward, *Tom Watson, Agrarian Rebel* (New York, 1938), 450, concludes, "If Watson had any hand in launching the new organization [the Klan], no record has been found that reveals it. Yet if any mortal man may be credited (as no one man may rightly be) with releasing the forces of human malice and ignorance and prejudice, which the Klan merely mobilized, that man was Thomas E. Watson."

6. The *Atlanta Constitution*, July 9, 1924, p. 1, notes that Forrest admitted to the authenticity of the document.

7. The *Atlanta Constitution*, June 27, 1924, p. 1, notes that at the Democratic national convention Cohen claimed that, to his knowledge, not one of the fifty-six delegates from Georgia was a Klansman.

8. Reuben Maury, *The Wars of the Godly* (New York, 1928), 285; Michael Williams, *The Shadow of the Pope* (New York, 1932), 141-42, are fully satisfied with the Klan's claim of responsibility for Underwood's political retirement. In evaluating the article by Evans in *The World's Work*, the *New York Times*, January 8, 1928, III, p. 1, contends that the secret order did not frighten the Senator out of politics; "What the masked gang did was to disgust Mr. Underwood, and to make him see the futility of further sacrifice of time, energy and health for a State rotten to the core with Klan influence."

9. McCall remained a Knight until October 19, 1927.

10. For a more detailed treatment of Graves' admission of association with the Klan, see below, 98.

11. It was alleged that Mayfield had resigned from the Klan in January, 1922.

12. For the text of a letter by Culberson to an influential constituent, in which he expressed hope that the state authorities would take immediate steps to destroy the Klan, see *Cong. Record*, 67 Cong., 3 Sess., 7996.

13. For the details of the elimination contest held by one of the local Klans in Texas, Dallas Klan No. 66, see *Senator From Texas,* 68 Cong., 1-2 Sess. (Washington, 1924), 376-77. A stenographic record of the hearings on alleged irregularities in the 1922 Texas senatorial race held before the Senate Committee on Privileges and Elections, May 8-December 18, 1924, this will be cited hereafter as *Mayfield Hearings.*

14. The total vote garnered by the pro-Klan candidates in the Democratic senatorial primary of July 22, 1922, was approximately 177,000, while that received by the anti-Klan candidates was over 328,000.

15. Probably feeling that to do so was unnecessary, Mayfield never mentioned the Klan in his campaign addresses.

16. Erwin J. Clark, who while he was serving as District Judge of the McLennan County Court at Waco in the early 1920's was a Great Titan of a Province of the Realm of Texas, affirmed that in 1922 Evans (at the time Exalted Cyclops of the local Klan in Dallas, he was soon to be Imperial Kligrapp and then Imperial Wizard) argued that the secret order simply had to concentrate behind Mayfield in the Democratic primary because the Klan needed to have a senator elected from Texas who was "in a position to get in touch with the big business of the country." who was "in line with the railroad interests," and who could "even approach Standard Oil." In *Mayfield Hearings,* 68.

17. In 1924 Henry admitted that he had joined the Klan in February, 1922, but later withdrew from it. In *Mayfield Hearings,* 46, 56.

18. *Mayfield Hearings,* 1A, 51, *passim.*

19. Among the other seven candidates in this primary were Lieutenant Governor T. W. Davidson and wealthy lumberman Lynch Davidson.

20. For a short and incisive analysis of the personality and abilities of James E. Ferguson, see Charles W. Ferguson, "James E. Ferguson," *Southwest Review,* October, 1924, pp. 32-33.

21. Robertson received 190,885 votes, while Mrs. Ferguson got 145,1.

22. The *New York Times,* August 31, 1924, VIII, p. 3, in an extended article on the personal qualities of Mrs. Ferguson, declares, "The campaign slogan, 'Me for Ma,' while effectual as a vote-getter, does not embody any term ever used familiarly in the Ferguson family. . . . The 'Ma' idea came from her initials, M. A. Ferguson, her ordinary signature. . . . 'Ma' is not the kind of term applicable to a woman possessing as much dignity as Mrs. Ferguson, . . . but she well knew the force of the homely appeal."

23. The *New York Times,* August 5, 1924, p. 16, in an editorial devastatingly satirizes Mrs. Ferguson's leaving the speechmaking to her husband.

24. Mrs. Ferguson received 427,225 votes, while Robertson got 337,832.

25. It should be noted, however, that in this election the Republican party of the solidly Democratic state of Texas polled the largest vote in its history. Although Mrs. Ferguson received 422,558 votes to Butte's 294,970, for many years prior to the 1924 election the Republican gubernatorial candidate had never polled more than 65,000 votes.

26. In Thomas J. Walsh Papers, Library of Congress.

27. In the "run-off" primary, held on August 28, Moody received 469,182 votes to Mrs. Ferguson's 247,100.

CHAPTER VI

1. The *Charleston News and Courier*, June 10, 1924, p. 1, declares that Watson "complimented" the work of the Invisible Empire in his home state by endorsing for Republican gubernatorial nominee in 1924 the same individual, Edward Jackson, whom the Klan ultimately "carried to triumph" in the intra-party contest, while the *Louisville Courier-Journal*, June 10, 1924, p. 3, maintains that the Senator was compelled by Grand Dragon Bossert to enter into a "gentlemen's agreement" with the Klan in Indiana to save his political machine from being taken over by the Knights of that state.

2. The *New York Times*, June 10, 1924, p. 3, emphasizes that the original statement endorsing Watson given out by Klan headquarters at the Hotel Statler was dictated by Milton Elrod, a publicity man for the order, who said Evans had fully authorized the statement after first conferring with Klan leaders regarding its content, and then insisting that it be repeated to him in final form to check thoroughly against errors.

3. In the alignment between the South and the East over the Klan issue at the Democratic national convention of 1924 the South was readily aided by the Middle West, the other great stronghold of Klanism during the 1920's.

4. Democratic National Committee, *Official Report of the Proceedings of the Democratic National Convention held in Madison Square Garden, New York City, June 24, 25, 26, 27, 28, 30, July 1, 2, 3, 4, 5, 7, 8 and 9, 1924* (Indianapolis, 1924), 95-103, contains the speech made by Forney Johnson of Birmingham, a leading lawyer of the South, in nominating Senator Oscar W. Underwood for the presidency, in which Johnson read to the convention the famous Underwood-prepared anti-Klan plank, patterned after the anti-Know-Nothing plank adopted by the Democratic national convention of 1856. (Underwood, it should be remembered, intended to make his appeal for the nomination on his stand for a vigorous anti-Klan plank.)

5. Erwin's remarks not only took the convention by surprise but roused it to a spirited demonstration, for it was naturally assumed that a Georgian would have spoken for the majority report.

6. During his speech in favor of the minority plank Bryan kept referring to the secret order as the "Kloo Klux Klan."

7. Because of the confusion and the closeness of the result of the first poll, Permanent Chairman Walsh had to order a recapitulation of the entire vote.

8. The minority plank on the League of Nations presented by Baker had already been rejected by the convention by a vote of 742½ to 353½.

9. Although *The Illinois Kourier*, June 20, 1924, p. 2, reports that "the grand Dragon Realm of Illinois . . . will go to New York to the Democratic convention to help protect the government from papal domination," there is no evidence that he (Palmer) ever arrived on the scene.

10. Many Democratic party workers believed that Davis' bringing up the Klan issue had a negative effect upon his battle for the presidency. Representative Cordell Hull of Tennessee, as Democratic national chairman in 1924, received quite a few letters attesting to this. One said, for example, "And why, tell me, did Davis after being the outcome and product of a long struggle on the K.K.K. issue and after a minority report had been defeated in the convention platform go beyond the work of the convention and declare against the Klan? That was

a mistake." In Cordell Hull Papers, Library of Congress. Davis' eagerness to eliminate the Klan issue quickly from the campaign is evidenced in his correspondence. In a letter to William Jennings Bryan, he declared that the Klan issue "would have continuously cropped out in the campaign, if it had not been disposed of, and I am hoping that I have said the last word necessary on the subject." In William J. Bryan Papers, Library of Congress.

11. On July 4, 1924, in Cleveland, Ohio, various agrarian and labor groups launched a third party that eagerly nominated LaFollette for the presidency and promptly chose Burton K. Wheeler, the Democratic Senator from Montana who had helped conduct the investigations of corruption in the Harding administration, for the vice-presidency. The platform of the Progressive party, written by LaFollette himself, called for reforms in the American government and economy.

12. Evans must have been referring to LaFollette's action in 1917, when he first led the resistance in the Senate to the arming of merchant ships, and then voted against a declaration of war on Germany.

CHAPTER VII

1. Representatives of the Klan, headed by Evans, had traveled also to Kansas City, Missouri, during the national convention of the Republican party, but had done nothing more than observe the proceedings.

2. One of the tactics of the Klan was to attempt to convince the delegates from the South that the appeal for religious toleration included in the speech delivered by Robinson as permanent chairman of the convention was an indication of a deep pro-Catholic bias.

3. For the text of the letter in full, see *Raleigh News and Observer*, October 9, 1928, pp. 1-2.

4. For a highly complimentary biographical sketch of Heflin, see *Washington, D. C. Fellowship Forum*, December 6, 1924, p. 4. For a quite condemnatory delineation of Heflin, see Allan A. Michie and Frank Ryhlick, *Dixie Demagogues* (New York, 1939), 142-58. Heflin was an individual of the most violent anti-Catholic persuasion. In Congress he spoke often and long-windedly against that faith: one time he proclaimed that a Catholic employee in the Treasury Department had been induced to engrave a rosary on the plate of the latest issue of the dollar bill; another time he was aghast that the green drapes in the President's room in the Capitol had been replaced by those of red, "the color of the Cardinals of the Roman Catholic Church"; on one occasion he thundered that a "Roman Catholic flag" had been flown above the American flag on two battleships during religious services. For examples of the many anti-Catholic addresses made by him on the floor of the Senate, see *Cong., Record,* 69 Cong., 2 Sess., 1701-02, 1835-41, 1843, 2210-23; 70 Cong., 1 Sess., 1868-74, 2613-15, 7948-49, 8049-ʳ 8057-58, 8505-06, 8937-42, 9155-57, 10079-86, 10209-11, 10214-16.

5. Students of the presidential election of 1928 disagree as to the relative importance of these factors contributing to Hoover's victory. See, for example, Charles Edward Merriam and Harold Foote Gosnell, *The American Party System* (New York, 1929), 326; Roy V. Peel and Thomas C. Donnelly, *The 1928 Campaign, An Analysis* (New York, 1931), 52; Edmund A. Moore, *A Catholic Runs for President, The Campaign of 1928* (New York, 1956), 195-96. It is important to note that none of these authors is willing to state positively what effect Klan

opposition to Smith had upon the results of the election. For a sampling of letters written just after the election by private citizens offering what they believed to be the reasons for Hoover's victory, see Josephus Daniels Papers, Library of Congress; George W. Norris Papers, Library of Congress; Thomas J. Walsh Papers, Library of Congress; Hoke Smith Papers, University of Georgia.

CHAPTER VIII

1. For a more detailed treatment of Heflin's opposition to Smith in 1928, see above, 89.

2. Sprigle won the Pulitzer Prize for this job of reporting.

3. Black's opponents were Thomas E. Kilby, former Governor; James J. Mayfield, retired State Supreme Court Justice; L. Breckinridge Musgrove, coal mine operator and member of the national board of the Anti-Saloon League; John H. Bankhead, corporation lawyer.

4. In the summer of 1926 a journalist named Robert B. Smith made the charge that the Invisible Empire had "definitely established itself" in the Senate. The exact numerical strength of the Klan bloc could not be determined, he explained, for it depended upon the varying strength of the order in the individual states and the proximity of election day. Although Smith doubted that any member of the Upper House was actually a Knight, he emphasized that with a realization of the power of the Klan at the ballot box, a number of senators were almost as responsive to the will of the Imperial Wizard and of the Grand Dragons of the states they represented in Congress as members of the order would be. The series of events that took place in the 1930's involving Black and Heflin indeed lends credence to Smith's assertions regarding the Senate.

5. Graves was an officer in the famed Rainbow Division during World War I.

6. Graves' opponents were Charles S. McDowell, Lieutenant-Governor; Andrew G. Patterson, president of the State Public Service Commission; and Archie H. Carmichael, former state legislator.

7. These few remarks can mean nothing other than that Graves was at the time the Exalted Cyclops of the local Klan in Montgomery, Alabama.

8. It should be noted, however, that Communist organizers were able eventually to gain tremendous influence in a few unions, such as that of the electrical workers and longshoremen.

9. For a highly unfavorable character analysis of Colescott, see Heywood Broun, "Up Pops the Wizard," *The New Republic*, June 21, 1939, 186-87.

CHAPTER IX

1. For a quite uncomplimentary delineation of Green, see Roi Ottley, "I Met the Grand Dragon," *The Nation*, July 2, 1949, pp. 10-11.

2. In August, 1946, Assistant Attorney-General Daniel Duke was sent to New York and New Jersey to confer with Attorneys-General Nathaniel Goldstein and Walter D. Van Riper regarding the methods they had used in revoking the charters of the Klan in their states.

3. Green always insisted that among his patients were both Negroes and whites, both Protestants and non-Protestants.

4. It was out of respect for Spinks' ardent wish that the headship of the order was redundantly entitled.

5. Of the journalistic treatments of the White Citizens Council, one of the best is John Bartlow Martin, *The Deep South Says "Never,"* (New York, 1957).

6. Most of Kasper's colleagues in the White Citizens Council, by the way, deplored his background and tactics. Kasper had been born in New Jersey, attended Columbia University, run a bookstore specializing in anti-Semitic literature in Greenwich Village, where he associated with Negroes of both sexes. He had to face both state charges of sedition and incitement to riot and federal charges of contempt of court for interfering in September, 1956, with desegregation in the public high school in Clinton, Tennessee.

7. This order is not to be confused with the Association of Carolina Klans of the late 1940's and early 1950's led by Grand Dragon Thomas L. Hamilton.

8. In September, 1958, Governor Orval E. Faubus of Arkansas said that he was not in sympathy with the Klan and its methods, but that he would not use his office to interfere with the organization in his state so long as its members obeyed the law. In September of the previous year, it was the Governor who had obstructed desegregation in Central High School in Little Rock, by ordering National Guardsmen to surround the building and prevent the Negro students from entering.

9. The Citizens for Religious Freedom was founded in September, 1960, in Washington, D. C., at a meeting of 175 prominent Protestant ministers and laymen. The group issued a statement questioning whether any Catholic should be president. Two leading figures of the session were Dr. Norman Vincent Peale of New York's Marble Collegiate Church, a well-known author and columnist, and Dr. Daniel Poling, editor of the influential Protestant monthly, *Christian Herald.* Peale, however, soon withdrew from the Citizens for Religious Freedom, telling his congregation that he had been "stupid" to associate with it.

10. Nixon obviously did not welcome the endorsement.

11. Six of Alabama's eleven Democratic electors and all of Mississippi's eight ran unpledged, but later agreed to support Senator Harry F. Byrd in the Electoral College.

INDEX

Ahoskie, North Carolina, 44, 133-34 n.5
Akron, Ohio, 103
Alabama, 5-6, 10, 13, 28, 47, 58, 64-66, 87, 89, 94-95, 97, 98, 101-02, 109, 110, 113, 115-19, 121-124, 127, 134 n.8 ch. V, 138 n.7, 139 n.11
Albany, New York, 89
Aldredge, S. R., 54
"alienism," 88, 89, 91, 101, 104, 124, 125
Allen, Louis C., 88
Allen, Stanton, 52
Alley, J. P., 133 n.4
Allied Klans, 115
American Federation of Labor, 102-03
American Labor party, 95
American Legion, 110
American Mercury, 57
American Protective Association, 133 n.11
American Protestant, 95
Americanism, Klan on, 15, 19-23, 49, 62, 83, 89, 90, 101, 107, 116, 124
Anderson, South Carolina, 94
Anderson County, South Carolina, 96
anti-prohibition, *see* prohibition
Anti-Saloon League, 91, 125
anti-Semitism, *see* Jews
Ardery, William B., 112-13
Arkansas, 13, 49-51, 64, 81, 90, 115, 124, 127, 134 n.10 ch. IV, 139 n.8
Arlington County, Virginia, 88
Arnall, Ellis, 113
Asheville, North Carolina, 34
Association of Arkansas Klans, 124
Association of Carolina Klans, 116, 118, 139 n.7
Association of Georgia Klans, 108-09, 114-15, 116, 117-18, 122

Association of South Carolina Klans, 123, 128
Atlanta, Georgia, 1, 6, 9-11, 23, 31, 46, 63, 88-89, 93, 94, 99, 103, 104, 105, 106, 108, 109, 111, 113-14, 120, 131 n.14
Augusta, Maine, 82
Austin, Texas, 53, 71

B. F. Goodrich Company, 103
Bain, Edgar H., 44
Baker, Newton D., 77, 136 n.8
Baker, William T., 42
Baltimore, 90, 95, 106
Baltimore Sun, 81
Bankhead, John H., 95, 138 n.3 ch. VIII
Baptists, 91, 111, 115, 122, 124, 126, 133 n.12
Barnard, Elmo C., 124
Barnes, J. A., 52
Barrs, Homer, 121
Bartlett, Texas, 52
Bartow, Florida, 104
Baton Rouge, Louisiana, 124
Beaumont, Texas, 51-52
Beavers, James L., 46
Bell, Edward Price, 31, 35
Bickley, James H., 122
Birmingham, Alabama, 6, 28, 64, 97, 98, 101-02, 109, 116, 119
"Birth of a Nation," 16, 132 n.4
Black, Hugo L., 65, 92, 95, 96-98, 138 nn.3 ch. VIII, 4
Blake, Aldrich, 17
Borland, Charles B., 40
Bossert, Walter F., 74-75, 80, 82, 136 n.1
Boston, Massachusetts, 64
boycotting, 12, 25-26, 118, 123
Boykin, John A., 46
Bradford County, Florida, 100

140

148   THE KU KLUX KLAN IN POLITICS